MORE REAL CHARACTERS

MORE REAL CHARACTERS

J. Vernon McGee

THOMAS NELSON PUBLISHERS
Nashville • Atlanta • London • Vancouver

Published in Nashville, Tennessee, by Thomas Nelson, Inc., and distributed in Canada by Word Communications, Ltd., Richmond, British Columbia, and in the United Kingdom by Word (UK), Ltd., Milton Keynes, England.

Scripture quotations are from the NEW KING JAMES VERSION of the Bible. Copyright © 1979, 1980, 1982, 1988 Thomas Nelson, Inc., Publishers.

Library of Congress Cataloging-in-Publication Data

McGee, J. Vernon (John Vernon), 1904–1988
    More real characters / J. Vernon McGee.
        p.   cm.
    ISBN 0-7852-7172-4
    1. Bible—Biography. I. Title.
BS571.M252   1997
220.9'2—dc21
[B]   96–50886
                                                          CIP

Printed in the United States of America

1 2 3 4 5 6 7 BVG 03 02 01 00 99 98 97

CONTENTS

FOREWORD

J. Vernon McGee's love for the Word of God was greatly enhanced by the individuals he encountered on its pages. He spent much time with them, analyzing their lives and their experiences with the God who loved them.

In fact, they became so real to him that he felt he even knew how they looked—and wished he were a portrait artist so you and I could also see them as they really were!

As you glance over the names and read the stories of the folk who comprise this second volume of *Real Characters*, you may wonder, *why these*? What did God see in their lives that He considered essential for us to know?

We trust that the Spirit of God will satisfy your heart with His own answers to this question as you enjoy, with Vernon McGee, *More Real Characters*.

Compiled and edited by Trude Cutler
Thru the Bible Radio Network

— 1 —

ISAAC AND REBEKAH

The Bridegroom and the Bride

The story of the choosing of a bride for Isaac is, in my opinion, one of the loveliest love stories ever recorded either in Scripture or out of Scripture. It has a bewitching charm, a sweet pathos, and a strange fascination as we read it again and again. The twenty-fourth chapter of Genesis, all sixty-seven verses, tells their story in a running narrative. You might like to read it in its entirety after this introduction, but right now let me quote parts of it to get the story before us:

Now Abraham was old, well advanced in age; and the LORD had blessed Abraham in

all things. So Abraham said to the oldest servant of his house, who ruled over all that he had, "Please, put your hand under my thigh, and I will make you swear by the LORD, the God of heaven and the God of the earth, that you will not take a wife for my son from the daughters of the Canaanites, among whom I dwell; but you shall go to my country and to my family, and take a wife for my son Isaac." And the servant said to him, "Perhaps the woman will not be willing to follow me to this land. Must I take your son back to the land from which you came?" But Abraham said to him, "Beware that you do not take my son back there. The LORD God of heaven, who took me from my father's house and from the land of my family, and who spoke to me and swore to me, saying, 'To your descendants I give this land,' He will send His angel before you, and you shall take a wife for my son from there. And if the woman is not willing to follow you, then you will be released from this oath; only do not take my son back there."
(Genesis 24:1–8)

Now let's drop down to verse 10:

Then the servant took ten of his master's camels and departed, for all his master's goods were in his hand. And he arose and went to Mesopotamia, to the city of

Nahor. And he made his camels kneel down outside the city by a well of water at evening time, the time when women go out to draw water. Then he said, "O LORD God of my master Abraham, please give me success this day, and show kindness to my master Abraham. Behold, here I stand by the well of water, and the daughters of the men of the city are coming out to draw water. Now let it be that the young woman to whom I say, 'Please let down your pitcher that I may drink,' and she says, 'Drink, and I will also give your camels a drink,'—let her be the one You have appointed for Your servant Isaac. And by this I will know that You have shown kindness to my master." And it happened, before he had finished speaking, that behold, Rebekah, who was born to Bethuel, son of Milcah, the wife of Nahor, Abraham's brother, came out with her pitcher on her shoulder. Now the young woman was very beautiful to behold, a virgin; no man had known her. And she went down to the well, filled her pitcher, and came up. And the servant ran to meet her and said, "Please let me drink a little water from your pitcher." So she said, "Drink, my lord." Then she quickly let her pitcher down to her hand, and gave him a drink. And when she had finished giving him drink, she said, "I will draw water for your camels also, until they have finished

drinking." Then she quickly emptied her pitcher into the trough, ran back to the well to draw water, and drew for all his camels. And the man, wondering at her, remained silent so as to know whether the LORD had made his journey prosperous or not.
(Genesis 24:10–21)

Now the servant comes into the home of Nahor. Right away he tells his story, how he's come to look for a bride for his master's son. Skipping down to verse 50 we read:

Then Laban and Bethuel answered and said, "The thing comes from the LORD; we cannot speak to you either bad or good. Here is Rebekah before you; take her and go, and let her be your master's son's wife, as the LORD has spoken." And it came to pass, when Abraham's servant heard their words, that he worshiped the LORD, bowing himself to the earth. Then the servant brought out jewelry of silver, jewelry of gold, and clothing, and gave them to Rebekah. He also gave precious things to her brother and to her mother. And he and the men who were with him ate and drank and stayed all night. Then they arose in the morning, and he said, "Send me away to my master." But her brother and her mother said, "Let the young woman stay with us a few days, at least ten; after that

she may go." And he said to them, "Do not hinder me, since the LORD has prospered my way; send me away so that I may go to my master." So they said, "We will call the young woman and ask her personally." Then they called Rebekah and said to her, "Will you go with this man?" And she said, "I will go." So they sent away Rebekah their sister and her nurse, and Abraham's servant and his men. And they blessed Rebekah and said to her:

"Our sister, may you become the mother of thousands of ten thousands; and may your descendants possess the gates of those who hate them."

Then Rebekah and her maids arose, and they rode on the camels and followed the man. So the servant took Rebekah and departed. Now Isaac came from the way of Beer Lahai Roi, for he dwelt in the South. And Isaac went out to meditate in the field in the evening; and he lifted his eyes and looked, and there, the camels were coming. Then Rebekah lifted her eyes, and when she saw Isaac she dismounted from her camel; for she had said to the servant, "Who is this man walking in the field to meet us?" The servant said, "It is my master." So she took a veil and covered herself. And the servant told Isaac all the things that he had done. Then Isaac

brought her into his mother Sarah's tent; and he took Rebekah and she became his wife, and he loved her. So Isaac was comforted after his mother's death.
(Genesis 24:50–67)

As I said before, this is one of the loveliest stories that is told on the pages of Scripture. Yet Isaac is one of the characters in the Word of God who does not appear, at first glance, to be a very impressive figure. He doesn't seem to be an outstanding personality.

However, if you lift him out of Scripture and make a careful and detailed study of him, you will find he is a central figure, a very famous person, and actually is outstanding as far as the Word of God is concerned. You'll find that he is always linked with his father Abraham, and the writer to the Hebrews explains it is because God said, "In Isaac your seed shall be called" (Hebrews 11:18); that is, the genealogy is always reckoned from Abraham to Isaac. His story is a thrilling story, even from his birth. He was born by a miracle. You remember, I'm sure, that when the messenger came from the Lord and announced to Abraham that he was to have a son and ninety-year-old Sarah was to be the mother, she laughed—she thought it just could not be. But,

By faith Sarah herself also received strength to conceive seed, and she bore a child when she was past the age, because she judged Him faithful who had promised.
(Hebrews 11:11)

When the child was born he was named Isaac, and *Isaac* means "laughter." He was a little bundle of joy. Aren't they all when they first come into the home! Chances are you remember a little bundle of joy who came into your home. But Isaac's birth was a miracle, and this child brought both joy and laughter into the home of Abraham.

Then, when Isaac was about thirty-three years of age (some scholars think he may have been only twenty-five, so somewhere between twenty-five and thirty-three), God commanded Abraham to offer this boy upon the altar! Then Abraham took him, his only begotten son, to offer as a sacrifice on an altar. As far as Abraham was concerned, he was a dead boy. The writer of the Book of Hebrews says he did it "concluding that God was able to raise him up, even from the dead, from which he also received him in a figurative sense" (Hebrews 11:19).

Another very interesting event, in fact the most conspicuous feature in Isaac's life, is the manner in which he got his wife. Very little Scripture is devoted to Isaac's life, but the entire twenty-fourth chapter of Genesis tells this remarkable story of his getting a bride.

And so we have the record of this man's life given in those three events that are said to be the most important events of our lives: birth, marriage, and death. All three are recorded concerning Isaac.

THE SERVANT'S COMMISSION

The way Isaac got a wife reminds us of Another who is yet to take a bride. It is a marvelous picture of the relationship of Christ and His church.

You remember Abraham called his servant and sent him yonder to Mesopotamia to find a wife for Isaac. We do not know the name of this servant. We believe it was Eliezer, the one who had charge of his household; but his name is not given here because it's not necessary. He has not gone on his own business or to get a bride for himself. He has not gone to talk about himself. He has gone to talk about another.

One of the figures of speech used in the New Testament is that the church is someday to become the bride of Christ. The Spirit of God, like this servant of Abraham, has come to talk about Another. Our Lord Jesus promised that He would send the Holy Spirit into the world and that when He would come He would not speak of Himself. "He will glorify Me, for He will take of what is Mine and declare it to you" (John 16:14). After all, the Holy Spirit, as far as we are concerned, is nameless. Tell me, what is the name of the third person of the Godhead? You say Holy Spirit, but that's not a name. It's merely a designation and title. We really don't know Him by name. He's the third person of the Godhead. We have God the Father; we have God the Son. But who is this third person? You say He is God the Holy Spirit. Well, that's all we know. He hasn't come to speak of Himself. He has come to speak of Another.

Now let's look back at the narrative. Abraham is sending his servant back to the old hometown to choose a bride for his son Isaac. Candidly, he did not want Isaac to marry one of the daughters of the Canaanites, a people given over to idolatry and paganism. Abraham wanted Isaac's bride to be a woman from among his own people back in the land of Haran. He didn't send Isaac himself, and there's nothing strange about that because parents always made the choice in that day.

We shall see that this choice of a bride is a marvelous picture of the Lord Jesus Christ securing His bride, the church. You see, the Holy Spirit has come into the world to get a bride; and that bride, my friend, must be made up of children of God—those who have been regenerated and given a capacity for heaven and the things of heaven. And so He's come into the world for that purpose.

The servant of Abraham had a heavy assignment, didn't he? It was up to him to get a bride for somebody else! Actually, the last thing I'd want to do would be to get a mate for another person. I talked to a girl for another fellow once, and I'll never get in that awkward position again! Somehow I just couldn't put my heart into it when I was asking her to marry somebody else. So I marvel at this servant in his tremendous undertaking because he is going to put all of his heart and all of his soul into it.

He leaves the home of Abraham in the land of the Canaanites and goes to northern Mesopotamia, to the city of Nahor near where Abraham had come from. He doesn't know just where to go, but as he moves along he comes to a well in the early evening, the time when women go out to draw water. The servant knows it's the area where Abraham had come from, but he doesn't know who's there. So he stops at this well, and he asks for God's help. This is a tremendous prayer:

Then he said, "O LORD God of my master Abraham, please give me success this day, and show kindness to my master Abraham. Behold, here I stand by the well of water, and the daughters of the men of the city are coming out to draw water. Now let it be that the young woman to whom I say, 'Please let down your pitcher that I may drink,' and she says, 'Drink, and I will also give your camels a drink'—let her be the one You have appointed for Your servant Isaac. And by this I will know that You have shown kindness to my master." (Genesis 24:12–14)

If he asks her for a drink and she responds graciously, well, it'll mean that she's polite. And then if she offers to water the camels, that means she's an extra special girl; and he will know she is the one God has chosen. And before he has finished praying, here she comes. It's Rebekah. She's a very beautiful girl—Scripture says so; and the Word of God never apologizes for that. We've got a notion in America today that only the devil can use beauty. May I say that God created it and can use it as well. You'll find many places in His Word where it says this girl or that girl was good to look at. And I think the Spirit of God knows when one's good-looking, my friend! And Rebekah must have been beautiful. I want you to get acquainted with her a little here because later on you'll read a story that may give the wrong impression concerning her, but here she's very attractive.

Rebekah comes out to the well and very modestly

doesn't say anything to the stranger. So he runs to her and asks, "May I please drink a little water from your pitcher." She's very polite so she says, "Why, yes!" And then she adds, "I will draw water for your camels also, until they have finished drinking." Now remember, friend, there are ten camels! I don't know how long it had been since they had last filled up, but camels have a very large capacity! And then you notice the man wondering at her. But he holds his peace, waiting to know whether the Lord has made his journey prosperous or not. You see the wisdom and the patience of this man. He doesn't move hurriedly at this juncture; he's waiting there upon God. He stands there and just watches all of this—thinking, *This is working out just exactly the way I prayed! I wonder if God is actually in this. Is this the girl for Isaac?* So he watches her as she moves about getting water for the camels.

Now I don't *know* this, but in my imagination I sometimes have to fill in Scripture. If I were an artist, there's not a character in the Bible I couldn't paint. I have visualized them, and I feel I know how Rebekah looked. I don't think she was a very large person—probably rather small with great big brown eyes. And did she have a mind of her own! You'll see that soon. As this girl moved back and forth from well to watering trough, the servant thought, *My, a wisp of a girl, and look how active she is and how beautiful she is! And polite! I wonder if this is the way God is leading. I do want to get the very best for Isaac.* So when she finishes watering, he gives her a gift and asks whose daughter she is and whether her family has room for them to spend the night. She assures him that they do and goes home to tell her father and brother.

We read that as the servant stands there, he bows down his head and worships the Lord. He knows now that he is in the will of God and that he is experiencing His clear leading in his life.

May I say to you, friend, if you are a Christian and you do not know what it is to have the clear leading of God, especially in critical circumstances, you have missed the greatest thrill of your life! I feel sorry for Christians who are always asking, "How can I find God's will for my life?" My friend, I hope you have gotten into a position where you have the clear leading of God. There's nothing more satisfying than that. Notice this servant of Abraham, uncertain at first and moving carefully, rather gingerly; but now he's sure.

And he said, "Blessed be the LORD God of my master Abraham, who has not forsaken His mercy and His truth toward my master."

Now here's the secret:

"As for me, being on the way, the LORD led me to the house of my master's brethren." (Genesis 24:27)

My friend, if you wait until you get into trouble, it's different. I counseled with a young married woman the other day. She said, "I'm seeking the Lord's will."

"Did you seek it when you got married?"

"No."

"Well, you have to be *on the way* for the Lord to lead you. I do not think you can expect someone to say 'hocus pocus' and straighten out in fifteen minutes of counseling a mistake that you've been spending all your life creating."

May I say, friend, it's when you and I are on the way and walking in fellowship with Him that the Lord leads us. When you are way out on the periphery of life and far from God, you cannot expect Him to come in all of a sudden and shine light upon your pathway. Abraham's servant said, "As for me, being on the way, the LORD led me. . . ." What a thrilling experience for this servant as he's just following through with his assignment. He does not know yet what the outcome will be, but obviously the outcome is going to be good because he has the leading of the Lord.

So standing there by the camels at the well he is thinking, *I'm going to let God work this thing out*. And before long here comes Laban, the brother of Rebekah. You see, this servant has come from Abraham, and Abraham was like a John D. Rockefeller and Henry Ford rolled into one. He was a wealthy man. His servant has given Rebekah earrings and bracelets of solid gold! If you know anything about Laban, you know he's a schemer. When he saw all of that jewelry he said, "Say, that's the fellow we want to entertain!" And so Laban comes out to meet him, and he says, "Come in, O blessed of the LORD! Why do you stand outside?" In other words, "Brother, come on home with us. We want to entertain you."

However, I tell you, Abraham's servant has a real mission.

I want you to notice his urgency now that he has God's mind in the matter. When "food was set before him to eat" (they have prepared a meal and are urging him to eat) he responds, "I will not eat until I have told about my errand." I think it is Father Bethuel who says, "Go ahead. If it's that urgent that you're putting it before your meal, then let's hear it. It must be important." So the servant tells his story. It is a thrilling story, by the way. It is the story of how God has led him. He begins like this, "I am Abraham's servant. . . ." He doesn't even give his own name. We'll see why as we go along.

He tells about his master Abraham who is, after all, related to Bethuel. And he tells about how, after Abraham had left that land and gone into Canaan, God had blessed him; how he had become a great man, a wealthy man in that area; and how in his old age God had given him a son through a miracle. And believe me, the servant makes that very clear. He tells how, when Abraham was a hundred years old and his wife Sarah was ninety years old, Isaac was born through a miracle of God. He tells the story, and they listen intently. Then he tells about how that boy Isaac, the only begotten son of the father, grew up and how, when he got to be around thirty-three years of age, God commanded that he be offered on an altar; and he tells how Abraham and Isaac, father and son, went together up the mountain to the place God had appointed.

Then they came to the place of which God had told him. And Abraham built an altar

there and placed the wood in order; and he bound Isaac his son and laid him on the altar, upon the wood.
(Genesis 22:9–10)

Bethuel knows Abraham well because he is his nephew, the son of Abraham's brother Nahor. I have a notion that at this point of the story Bethuel says, "I remember that Abraham would follow through with anything. I remember the day he told us God had called him to leave Ur of the Chaldees. And later when he was to leave Haran, we tried to dissuade him because he didn't even know where he was going. But he said God had called him, and none of us could stop him. And I tell you, if he said God told him to offer that boy, we know Abraham went through with it." Then the servant says, "But God stopped him! He wouldn't permit him to go through with it."

But the Angel of the LORD called to him from heaven and said, "Abraham, Abraham!" So he said, "Here I am." And He said, "Do not lay your hand on the lad, or do anything to him; for now I know that you fear God, since you have not withheld your son, your only son, from Me."
(Genesis 22:11–12)

God gave that boy back to him from the dead in a sense. Now the servant continues: "My master's wife is dead, and he is left alone. He's an old man, and he sent me to get a bride for his son. I have prayed, and God has brought me here. Now I wonder how you feel about it. If you think God is leading, then I'll take the girl back to Isaac. But if you think it's not the leading of God, then I'll go my way and find someone else because I know God must have someone in mind."

I think Laban looks at his father and his father looks at Laban and they look around, and over yonder in the shadows stands a girl with big brown eyes. She had listened to all of this—Isaac's miraculous birth, how he was offered on the altar, how he was brought back from the dead, how he is the heir of all things, and how the servant is looking for a bride to be a joint heir with Isaac. She's listening. And so Rebekah's father and brother, Bethuel and Laban, talk it over. "Well, what can we say? If God's doing this, we don't want to stand in the way." So they say to the servant, "As far as we're concerned, if God is leading, then you can take Rebekah and go."

REBEKAH'S CHOICE

The next morning the servant says, "I want to pack up and leave." But they object, "Wait a minute! Let her stay a little while, at least ten days." The mother comes up and says, "We can't just send our daughter away today. Give us ten more days to get ready." The servant says, "No, it will have to be today." And the father says, "Well, the thing to do is to ask Rebekah." So they call Rebekah and bring her in. You know I said before that she was a straightforward girl with a will. When they ask her, "Will you go with this man?" she answers, "I will go." She has made up her mind already. "I heard about how wonderful he is. I'll go." Oh, she has been won; not by the bridegroom but by the servant.

I like that girl. And I want to tell you, she has made a forthright decision. There is no beating around the bush here. This girl has made a decision.

Beloved, after the Lord Jesus returned to heaven's glory, He sent the Holy Spirit to earth as He had promised. The Holy Spirit has come from heaven into this world with the assignment of calling out a bride for the Son of God. The church is to be the bride of Christ, and she is to be presented to Him someday.

Sometimes I think we give the wrong impression. I'm not sure the Holy Spirit is begging us to come to Christ as some folks seem to indicate. He is presenting the claims of the Son. He is declaring that He was virgin born, that He died on the cross, and that He rose again from the dead. He is saying that the Son is to inherit all things. Now the Holy Spirit is asking us, "Do you want to come along? If you don't, I'll go down and talk to your neighbor, because I'm calling out a bride. I'm calling out those who constitute this body of believers spoken of as the bride of Christ to be presented to their heavenly Bridegroom someday."

I thank God for Rebekah, this young woman who said, "I will go." Peter, speaking of Christ in his first epistle, wrote, "Whom having not seen you love" (1 Peter 1:8). Oh, these pussyfooting folk, these lackadaisical folk, these people in our churches who want to be conservative and want to be liberal at the same time, who don't want to take a stand for God, who don't want to come out and accept Christ. "I'll go," Rebekah said. And, friend, if you won't go, the Holy

Spirit will invite somebody else because He's calling out a bride for the Son of God! And He's telling you about the Son, how wonderful He is.

A young lady who came in to talk to me some time ago said, "There are two young men who are interested in me." She told me about one; she told me about the other. Then she said, "I do not know which one to choose and thought maybe you might help me."

I said to her, "Do you know a third boy? If you do, you'd better start dating him. Because if you are in a position where you don't know which one it is, it's neither one of those boys! You will know him when he comes along. You'll *know*."

Oh, these people today who are standing on the sidelines. "Yes," they agree, "Jesus is wonderful." But have they ever said to Him, "I'll go with You"? Have *you* ever yet made a decision for Him? I like Rebekah. She hasn't even seen Isaac, yet she says, "I will go. I'll be his bride."

So the servant and his men, with Rebekah and her maids, begin the journey that very day. They start out across the desert wilderness. Have you ever seen pictures of that desert stretching from the land of Haran and into Palestine? It was as dry then as it is today. It was a long, arduous journey, and they were in constant danger from enemies on every hand. It was a trip filled with hardships. And, friend, I can testify that riding a camel is not easy! On a visit to Egypt, a friend and I took a camel ride from our rented house to the big pyramid. I think we rode a little over a mile, but it seemed like five miles. I found out the reason camels are called "ships of the desert"—it will make you seasick riding one! And you should have seen us dismounting! They're not easy to ride by any means, and I can well imagine Rebekah spending several weeks going across that desert. The caravan couldn't travel many miles a day, just from one oasis to another. It was difficult; it was monotonous, rugged, and stressful. As they went along I think Rebekah got travel weary.

After a long, hot day's journey they would come to an oasis in the evening. A fire is built because in the desert it gets cold after sundown. As they sit around the fire, Rebekah is weary and perhaps homesick and maybe a little discouraged. And then she says to the servant, "Tell me again about Isaac. What was it you said about his birth? Tell me about the time his father took him yonder to the mount as a sacrifice. Tell me about how wonderful he is." And the servant says, "But I told you all that last night." She says, "Yes, I know, but I want to hear about it again." So he tells it again. And the next night, after a very tiring and exacting day when they all are weary, the servant wants to go to bed; but Rebekah says, "Wait a minute before you leave. Tell me about the time when he was offered on the altar." And he says, "My, I must have told that story to you a hundred times." But she wants to hear it again. I think she must have inspired the song, "Tell me the old, old story of Jesus and His love."

The next morning she's up bright and early. She says, "Let's be on our way." Perhaps the citizens of the desert, as she passes through, are impressed, saying, "This girl means business. It must be a wonderful man she's going to meet!" I'm not sure but what some of them would have liked to have gone along.

One of the reasons today that the world outside is not impressed with the Lord Jesus Christ is because *we* are not impressed. We are not living in anticipation of meeting our heavenly Bridegroom. We are too busy planting flowers in this world. Dr. George Gill, in his very courteous and lovely manner, used to say—and it was startling coming from him—"The church is making the world a better place for people to go to hell in!" And that's what some of us are doing. Although Rebekah hadn't seen Isaac, she loved him already. And the apostle Peter writes to you and me: "whom having not seen you love. Though now you do not see Him, yet believing, you rejoice with joy inexpressible and full of glory" (1 Peter 1:8).

We are pilgrims and strangers in this world today, my beloved, and the going gets rough at times. The only solution is to come back to the old, old story of Jesus and His love. May I say, that's the thing that kept this girl going yonder to the promised land.

ISAAC MEETS HIS BRIDE

Then the day came, and what a day! We're told here,

Now Isaac came from the way of Beer Lahai Roi, for he dwelt in the South. And Isaac went out to meditate in the field in the evening; and he lifted his eyes and looked, and there, the camels were coming.
(Genesis 24:62–63)

And the word was passed along, "The camels are coming! The camels are coming!" The servant is coming home with the bride for Isaac!

Then Rebekah lifted her eyes, and when she saw Isaac she dismounted from her camel; for she had said to the servant, "Who is this man walking in the field to meet us?" The servant said, "It is my master." So she took a veil and covered herself.
(Genesis 24:64–65)

The journey's over now. The man whom Rebekah sees is to be her lover, her husband, and her lord.

We sometimes talk a great deal about wanting to be alive when the Lord Jesus comes again. Most of us have no desire to go through the doorway of death. I wish the Lord would come, and I can be honest and sincere and say I wish He would come tonight. I do wish it with all my heart. But if you have a notion that just to be alive when the Lord comes means that you will be in on the big end of the event, you're wrong. The big end takes place up yonder. What a thrill it's going to be! Do you notice that the wonderful climax of this story is given from the bridegroom's viewpoint? The word is passed along, "The camels are coming!" What excitement—the bride is coming!

Have you ever stopped to consider that today most of the church is already up yonder with Christ? We like to say, "Oh, my loved one, my poor loved one has died." Yes, but that "poor loved one" is lots better off than you are. And one of these days, when Jesus comes, what excitement there will be up there in heaven with Him! Do you know what all those up yonder who have gone on ahead will be saying? "My loved ones down yonder are coming home! The earthly trial is over. The desert journey is ended! They're coming home; my loved ones are coming!" You see, there are many more of them up there than there are down here today. What excitement there will be!

Dr. Bill Anderson, beloved pastor of the First Presbyterian Church in Dallas, Texas, was one of several prominent men who wanted so badly to see Christ come, but he was still in the prime of life when he died. Allen Fleece and I had been in Dallas Theological Seminary together during that time, and when we met years later we were talking about Dr. Bill, as we called him. I said, "I can't understand why God took him and those other men who really wanted to see Christ coming." And Allen said, "That's worried me too. But, Mac, it's up yonder where the fun is going to be." We think it will be wonderful to be alive down here when it happens—to be caught up to meet the Lord in the air—and we talk about that. But to be up yonder with Christ and then to come back to earth *with Him*, how wonderful that will be! Oh, my friend, the last contingent of the church is coming home. The body is to be made complete. And the bride is to be presented to the waiting Bridegroom! What a picture!

And you know what happens next.

Then Isaac brought her into his mother Sarah's tent; and he took Rebekah and

she became his wife, and he loved her. So Isaac was comforted after his mother's death.
(Genesis 24:67)

Rebekah found that Isaac was more wonderful than she ever dreamed he was! And, my friend, I don't know what you think of the Lord Jesus today; but whatever you think of Him now, He's lots more wonderful than that. Wait until you see Him! We are told that Rebekah, according to the custom of the East, had said to her maiden, "Get my veil!" And she covered her face to be presented to Isaac. Likewise, when we go into our Bridegroom's presence, we will have to be clothed with His righteousness. I tell you, friend, we can't go there in our own merit or our own ability. We'll have to go there clothed in the righteousness of Christ. And when we go into His presence clothed in His righteousness, what a glorious meeting it will be!

And then it says of Isaac, "He loved her." Isn't that wonderful? I'm looking forward to going to heaven, not only because I'm going to love everybody in heaven but also because everybody in heaven is going to love me! And, beloved, the most wonderful thing of all will be when you are with Him, the Son of God; you will be with the One who sincerely, devotedly, *loves* you. He demonstrated it when He was here. When you and I were sinners, unlovely and lost, He died for us, paid the penalty for our sins with His own life's blood. He did it because He loved us and wanted us to be with Him forever.

Abraham said, "Isaac must have a bride." And God said, "We must have redeemed sinners in heaven." What a glorious thing! And He will love us. He will love us throughout eternity! What a picture!

— 2 —

JOCHEBED
The Mother of Moses

When the question was asked on a quiz program, "Who was the mother of Moses?" not one contestant was able to give the correct answer. In fact, one of them suggested it was a trick question because he didn't think Moses' mother was even mentioned in the Bible. Let me ask *you* the question: Could you have named the mother of Moses? Well, Jochebed is the name of the mother of Moses, and the Word of God identifies her as such:

> **Now Amram took for himself Jochebed, his father's sister, as wife; and she bore him Aaron and Moses. . . .**
> (Exodus 6:20)

Jochebed is one of the greatest mothers mentioned in the Word of God. She rates right along with Sarah and

Rachel and Deborah and Ruth and Hannah and Mary the mother of Jesus and Eunice and Lois. She is, indeed, one of the great mothers of Scripture. In fact, she found a niche in the eleventh chapter of Hebrews, and many wonderful mothers missed having that distinction.

The Book of Exodus opens with the people of Israel in Egyptian bondage. They were no longer a slave minority, but actually outnumbered the Egyptian population at this time—which caused Egyptians to fear they would join forces with any invading army and fight against them in the event of war.

> **So Pharaoh commanded all his people, saying, "Every son who is born you shall cast into the river, and every daughter you shall save alive."**
> (Exodus 1:22)

At this time Moses was born to Amram and Jochebed. Notice what the Book of Hebrews says about it:

> **By faith Moses, when he was born, was hidden three months by his parents, because they saw he was a beautiful child; and they were not afraid of the king's command.**

Now this is Jochebed's verse:

> **By faith Moses, when he became of age, refused to be called the son of Pharaoh's daughter.**
> (Hebrews 11:23–24)

This is her place in the eleventh chapter of Hebrews. Though not mentioned by name, she is referred to here; and her importance is the fact that she was the guiding light in Moses' life during those formative years.

The life of Moses can be divided into three periods, three forty-year periods. The first forty years were spent in Egypt. The second forty were spent in Midian. The third period of forty years was spent at Sinai and around Mount Sinai in the wilderness. You can identify these three places like this: the first period was in the palace; the second in the desert; the third in the wilderness. In the first period he was *drawn out*. In fact, that's the meaning of his name. When the princess decided to keep him as her own ". . . she called his name Moses, saying, 'Because I drew him out of the water'"(Exodus 2:10). He was drawn out of the River Nile. The second period is the period of *discipline*. He was disciplined by God in that period. And then there is the third period. He was the man of God who *delivered* Israel.

I want you to notice that the first thing we're told is concerning his parents. "By faith Moses, when he was born, was hidden three months by his parents, because they saw he was a beautiful child; and they were not afraid of the king's command" (Hebrews 11:23). That has to do with the parents; but when I turn back to Exodus, the second chapter, I find out it was his mother who was the prime instigator in hiding him. It was his mother who made that little watertight ark to float him in and left him there among the reeds of the Nile River. It was his mother who had oversight in this particular period of his life.

May I say to you that it took real courage in that day to defy the edict of a pharaoh; and the one who would incur his wrath probably would suffer the death penalty. And certainly the life of the child would be snuffed out if he were found by an Egyptian.

Exodus gives us a good picture of Moses' mother:

So the woman conceived and bore a son. And when she saw that he was a beautiful child, she hid him three months.
(Exodus 2:2)

And that's been interesting to me. A proper or goodly child, or exceedingly fair as it is sometimes translated, means he was a beautiful child. Somebody says, "Well, after all, every mother thinks her child is beautiful." The child may look like the father and grandfather on the father's side put together, and the mother still thinks that little fellow is a beautiful child, you see. Well, what does that add to the story? It adds a great deal. It means that this mother believed that God would use her boy and that He would do something special with this little fellow. Although everything seemed to be against it at this time, she kept him hidden for three months. But after three months she couldn't hide him any longer. And the reason is obvious; his little lungs developed, and apparently Moses had a pretty good set of lungs. You must remember he spoke to thousands of people in the wilderness without a loudspeaker. And I have a notion at three months of age, though he might not have been able to speak to thousands of people, the neighborhood knew he was

there! It was obvious that something had to be done
about him. And I want you to notice what Jochebed
did.

Faith never is foolish, nor is it fanatical, although it's
called that in some circles. But Moses' mother was not
foolish or fanatical in what she did.

**But when she could no longer hide him,
she took an ark of bulrushes for him,
daubed it with asphalt and pitch, put the
child in it, and laid it in the reeds by the
river's bank.**
(Exodus 2:3)

Now she is doing this with great wisdom. She's not
exposing the child. She had been hiding him in their
home, but now she takes him down there by the river
and hides him among the reeds by the river's bank. Do
you suppose she had something in mind? I'm confident
that she was following a very careful plan. I wonder if
God had given her that plan. I think He did since
Hebrews 11:23 says that ". . . they were not afraid of
the king's command."

**And his sister stood afar off, to know what
would be done to him.**
(Exodus 2:4)

Miriam was part of the plan, you see. She was stationed at a distance, watching what would take place
because they knew Pharaoh's daughter would come
down to this particular spot to bathe, and they were

confident this would be their chance to save the baby's life. And may I say to you that this is now what concerns this wonderful mother—for she's just that. She knew that if God could bring together a woman's heart and a baby's cry, something wonderful might happen.

My friend, God uses those little things in life. As you go through the Word of God, you will find that God has changed the destinies of nations by small incidents like that. God uses those things.

Well, back there on the bank of the Nile River God did bring together a woman's heart and a baby's cry.

> **Then the daughter of Pharaoh came down to bathe at the river. And her maidens walked along the riverside; and when she saw the ark among the reeds, she sent her maid to get it. And when she opened it, she saw the child, and behold, the baby wept. So she had compassion on him, and said, "This is one of the Hebrews' children."**
> (Exodus 2:5–6)

And you know that Miriam had been instructed what to do when this happened, and she was right there and ready.

> **Then his sister said to Pharaoh's daughter, "Shall I go and call a nurse for you from the Hebrew women, that she may nurse the child for you?"**
> (Exodus 2:7)

Profane history tells us a great deal at this particular point. This Pharaoh's daughter did not have a son; so when she looked down into this little ark and saw Moses, an unusually fine-looking baby, she decided to keep him as her own son, thinking, *this is the one we'll train to be an Egyptian prince.* And so she said, "Yes, go get some nurse to take care of this baby." And you know who Miriam got. Miriam brought their own mother, Jochebed.

Then Pharaoh's daughter said to her, "Take this child away and nurse him for me, and I will give you your wages. . . ."
(Exodus 2:9)

Wages! Here's something that Jochebed would have been willing to do for nothing, but now she's going to be paid to openly take care of her own precious baby!

Here we begin the most important phase of Moses' life. I wonder if the life of Moses wasn't shaped more by his mother than was the life of any other man who ever lived on topside of this earth. No mother ever had the influence Jochebed had upon this boy as she raised him.

As I read the story, I think of another mother in Nazareth by the name of Mary who raised another little boy by the name of Jesus; and there's a striking similarity. But do you know what Jochebed had to do? She had to counteract all the influence of Egypt, and that influence was evil and it was godless. As I look yonder at that scene I see a little, weak woman—a slave in a foreign land; and over against that weakness

there is the power of Egypt. I'm no betting man, but if
I were, I would gamble on Egypt. I'd say that Egypt
will win, not that little woman; she's too weak. But
may I say to you, here's the story:

> **By faith Moses, when he became of age,
> refused to be called the son of Pharaoh's
> daughter, choosing rather to suffer afflic-
> tion with the people of God than to enjoy
> the passing pleasures of sin, esteeming the
> reproach of Christ greater riches than the
> treasures in Egypt. . . .**
> (Hebrews 11:24–26)

Moses at forty years of age made his choice. It says,
"When he became of age." It raises in my mind the
question of when is the age of accountability? I want to
say candidly that I do not know what the age of
accountability is. Now there are some people who think
I know, but I don't. I read in God's Word that the
Hebrew child at twelve years of age was set apart as a
man; but I also know that in the first chapter of the
Book of Numbers, when they were choosing soldiers, it
was "from twenty years old and above." Then I turn
over a few pages to the fourth chapter, and I read that
when God is choosing priests, He says, "from thirty
years old and above." Now here's Moses becoming of
age at forty years. When is the age of accountability?
twelve years? twenty years? thirty years? forty years?
You can pick any one of them. But the age of accountability is only incidental here. The important matter is
that the decision Moses made at forty years of age was

the decision that depended on the training he had received yonder at the knees of his mother, for everything else in his life was godless except that one woman. That one mother stood between God and hell, my friend, and she held the fort!

I look again at a scene down yonder in Egypt, and in the distance I see the pyramids; I see a civilization that compares favorably with our civilization today. I see a palace, and out yonder in the courtyard I see a woman who is dressed like an Egyptian servant. I see a little boy who is dressed like a prince. And all I can say is that I think she must be the nurse of that little boy. She must be raising a prince down there. He's to be the next pharaoh. I wonder what she's teaching him.

Now drawing near, I discover something I didn't notice at first. I see that there's a love in her eyes that no servant ever had for another's child. It's the love of a mother for her own little son. I see that the little boy is not an Egyptian, he's a Hebrew boy; and those two sure do look alike. Her boy. All Egypt is against her because they want to bring that little fellow up to be the next pharaoh. Her boy! I see her. I tell you, friend, I don't think she's got a ghost of a chance, just looking at it from the outside. I don't see how she can stand against all of that. First of all she has to counteract all the evil influence of Egypt, its pleasure and its sin. Listen to this:

By faith Moses, when he became of age, refused to be called the son of Pharaoh's daughter, choosing rather to suffer

affliction with the people of God than to enjoy the passing pleasures of sin.
(Hebrews 11:24–25)

There's pleasure in sin. The Word of God says there is. It's pretty brief, though: "At the last it bites like a serpent, and stings like a viper" (Proverbs 23:32). But it's there for awhile, and all of that pleasure is available to Moses. He can have anything in the world he wants in Egypt.

I see that mother there with her little boy. She is giving him a correct perspective on life. She's teaching him about eternal matters and about spiritual matters. She says to him, "Moses, even those pyramids out there won't stand because the sands of the Sahara Desert are going to blow in upon them and almost cover them up. But, Moses, there are certain things that are eternal." Later on Moses wrote a wonderful psalm, and I quote only one verse of it: "So teach us to number our days, that we may gain a heart of wisdom" (Psalm 90:12). When he was a little boy his mama was teaching him those things. Down yonder in Egypt she was the only bridge God had to reach Moses in those days. The bridge was Jochebed.

Then there is something else she taught him:

By faith he forsook Egypt, not fearing the wrath of the king; for he endured as seeing Him who is invisible.
(Hebrews 11:27)

She taught him about Abraham, Isaac, and Jacob. I imagine she said something like this: "Moses, you are

not a pharaoh and you're not an Egyptian. Your ances-
tor Abraham lived in Ur of the Chaldees, and he forsook all of that. God called him and he left it all":

**By faith Abraham obeyed when he was
called to go out to the place which he
would receive as an inheritance. And he
went out, not knowing where he was
going. By faith he dwelt in the land of
promise as in a foreign country, dwelling
in tents with Isaac and Jacob, the heirs
with him of the same promise; for he
waited for the city which has foundations,
whose builder and maker is God.**
(Hebrews 11:8–10)

Jochebed's instruction continued: "And then Isaac
came along after Abraham; and later Jacob, with all of
his sin, finally gave it all up and went looking for that
city. We were brought down here to Egypt, and God has
said that one of these days He is going to raise up a
deliverer, and we are to leave the land of Egypt. I've
always believed you would be the deliverer, Moses. You
are not a pharaoh. Be God's man."

"By faith Moses, when he became of age, refused to
be called the son of Pharaoh's daughter." Over against
all the idolatry of Egypt and its evil influence, this little mother stood there teaching this boy about the living and true God so that Moses could write later on,
"You shall have no other gods before Me" (Exodus
20:3). Moses had first learned this down in Egypt at his
mother's knee.

Wait, she didn't tell him only about Abraham, Isaac

and Jacob. We read in Hebrews 11:26, "esteeming the reproach of Christ greater riches than the treasures in Egypt . . ." You mean to tell me that Jochebed told Moses about Christ? I believe she did. I have no doubt that she told this little boy how God had promised to send a Savior into the world and that God had promised Abraham, "I will make you a blessing to all people." I have a notion she said something like this: "Moses, a Savior is coming! Maybe you, Moses, will be the deliverer to lead our people out of Egyptian slavery." You say to me today, "Are you sure about that?" Well, Moses made a hard choice on the basis that he was "esteeming the reproach of Christ greater riches than the treasures of Egypt." Also, when Moses was preparing Israel's new generation to enter the land of promise, he gave them this prophecy of Christ's coming:

The LORD your God will raise up for you a Prophet like me from your midst, from your brethren. Him you shall hear.
(Deuteronomy 18:15)

And note these words of Christ when He was here:

For if you believed Moses, you would believe Me; for he wrote about Me.
(John 5:46)

Will you look with me again into that palace in Egypt. It's nighttime, and Jochebed is putting the little fellow to bed. She's so frail, so weak; only a female slave. And I look yonder to Pharaoh on the throne, and I think how powerful he is. I see the influence of Egypt; and I see those pyramids out there, and I say, "All of this is tremendous!" She's nothing in the eyes of the world—nothing. But God has chosen the weak things of this world! And yonder when Moses came to forty years of age, this mature, fine-looking prince in Pharaoh's palace made a decision. He could say, "I'm turning my back on all this because my mother told me about things that are spiritual. I will not depart from them; I'll not give them up. I'm willing to give up everything in Egypt, but not my mother's God and the things that are eternal." Moses turned his back on all of it, my beloved. Jochebed *won*! She didn't lose; she won, my friend.

This week a lady who heard I was speaking on the mother of Moses sent me a poetic piece written years ago by Harriet W. Gillis and titled "Jochebed, a Mother." Listen to this:

She never heard of Mother's Day, nor ever felt the need. Content was she to train, to clothe her little world of three. How unpretentious! No career! Just answering childhood's questions, and telling of the Hebrews bold in faith and courage for the Lord. Of kissing bruises and washing tired, dirty feet, demanding prompt obedience and teaching prayer to God. Just homely tasks, but faithfully performed. Yes, done so well that nigh to forty years in Pharaoh's court could not erase the imprint

*made. And Moses made his choice because
long years before his mother had made hers!*

That's Jochebed. Yet few have ever heard of her.

May I say that Jochebed had to counteract all the
pagan culture, even religion and the godless education
of Egypt because, you see, Moses was trained in all of
those things. Again somebody says, "Are you sure of
that?" Yes. When Stephen was making his defense
before the Sanhedrin he said this:

**And Moses was learned in all the wisdom
of the Egyptians, and was mighty in words
and deeds.**
(Acts 7:22)

You see, he was to be trained as the pharaoh, and they
sent him away to college. In that day it was the Temple
of the Sun, and don't you look down upon it today. It
would compare favorably with our best universities.
They taught chemistry, and in that field of chemistry
they had an embalming process that we can't duplicate
today. And the colors yonder in the tombs of the kings
are as bright as if they were put on yesterday. May I say
to you, any paint company would like to get that for-
mula, and they would pay handsomely for it, my friend.
Moses was learned in all the wisdom of the Egyptians.
He knew its art, and its art was superb. He knew its
architecture, for it was also superb. He knew its
astronomy, and amazingly the Egyptians knew the distance to the sun. Moses knew mathematics, and today
our mathematics is built on what the Egyptians knew.

Their literature was extensive. They had one of the largest libraries the world has ever seen.

Moses was learned in all the wisdom of the Egyptians, and that little mother had to counteract all of that. It looked like she had failed. But when he was full forty years old, it came into his heart to visit his brethren, the children of Israel; and he thought that he was ready to deliver Israel. But forty years of training in Egypt wasn't enough for God, and God sent him out on the desert to train him for another forty years. But it must have looked to Jochebed as if she had failed.

By faith he forsook Egypt, not fearing the wrath of the king; for he endured as seeing Him who is invisible.
(Hebrews 11:27)

I think Jochebed felt she had lost him when he left Egypt. You see, Moses never mentions her again; and while Moses was away, evidently Jochebed died without seeing him again. And I have a notion that during those long years after he left, many a time she went to God in prayer and said, "Oh God, I've lost him. I've lost him. All those fruitless years of training. I tried my best to instill in him these wonderful principles. I told him about Abraham, Isaac, Jacob and Christ. I told him about all these things. It just didn't seem to yield any dividend at all." My friend, it *did* yield a dividend. Long after she was gone, Moses became God's instrument for the deliverance of His people. He was the one to whom God gave the first five books of Scripture that we have in our Bibles today—the Pentateuch. No mother who brings up a child in the discipline and instruction of the Lord can finally fail. She may die believing she has failed, but God will see that she doesn't fail.

There was yonder in London years ago a woman who took in washing. She had a boy by the name of John. He was John Newton. When he was young he ran away to sea, and he sank so low that he sold himself into slavery in Africa. Also he dabbled in the occult and degraded himself as low as any man could do. However, this man had a little, faithful mother who every day, over a scrub board in London, prayed for that boy and mingled her tears with the soapsuds. And one day he was converted to Christ! John Newton became a pastor and literally reached thousands of people through his wonderful hymns that we still sing. And among those thousands he reached was a cultured, refined, educated man by the name of Thomas Scott. No one believed that John Newton would ever reach Scott, but he did, and Scott turned to God. In turn, Scott began to reach many others; and one of them was a man completely different from him, a man by the name of William Cowper, a dyspeptic, sickly type of fellow, but a man who wrote,

> *There is a fountain filled with blood,*
> *Drawn from Immanuel's veins,*
> *And sinners plunged beneath that flood,*
> *Lose all their guilty stains.*

And Cowper touched a man by the name of William Wilberforce, one of the most brilliant politicians England ever had—a gambler, a drunkard—but

William Cowper reached him for Christ. And Wilberforce became a great lay preacher. Thousands came to
Christ. Why? Because a little mother, bent over a wash-
tub in London, held onto God and died believing she
had failed. I'd say she hadn't!

John Wesley's mother was Susannah Wesley. One
day her husband said to her, "You have spoken to that
boy nineteen times about the same thing." She said,
"The reason I spoke to him nineteen times was because
if I had not said it one more time, I would have failed.
So I just kept saying it." My, she was a poised mother!
Also she knew Hebrew, Greek, and Latin and taught
these to her boy, John Wesley. Oh, he got away from
God, left home, even went as a missionary before he
was converted. We like to speak of the night he went
yonder to a meeting in Aldersgate Street and listened
to the reading of Luther's preface to the Epistle to the
Romans. Concerning this experience he wrote: "I felt
my heart strangely warmed and I did trust in Christ,
Christ alone, for salvation. And an assurance was given
me that He had taken away my sins, even mine, and
saved me from the law of sin and death." My friend, it
was because he happened to have a mother, Susannah
Wesley, who brought him up in the discipline of the
Lord. She thought she had failed, but she did not fail!

Dr. C. I. Scofield, the editor of the *Scofield Reference
Bible,* which has been a great blessing to multitudes of
us, had been a drunken lawyer. That's one of the things
the critics of the *Scofield Bible* like to point out today.
They say, "It was produced by a man who was a
drunken lawyer!" True, he was. He was a failure—a
brilliant international lawyer, but alcohol got him. And

one day yonder in St. Louis he was led to Christ. He'd had a praying mother, but she had died. Mel Trotter tells of an incident when a few of them were having prayer together and Dr. Scofield suddenly interrupted his prayer with, "Oh, Lord, I don't know whether this could be or not, but if my mother doesn't know I'm converted, won't You tell her?" She knew her boy was a drunkard, and she died believing he never would be saved.

Mel Trotter also had a praying mother who had brought him up right, but he, too, became a drunkard as well as a thief and a pickpocket. But because his fingers were not as adept as they should have been under the influence of liquor, he was arrested one day and sent to Joliet prison and served time there. After he was paroled, he went to the south side of Chicago. One night after he had cleaned out the cuspidors in a cheap saloon and begged for a free beer to be given to him, the bartender finally said, "You're a nuisance. Why don't you go down to the river and jump in?" So he started walking down toward the river. He started, but one of the men at the Pacific Garden Mission steered him into the service that was in progress, and Mel Trotter turned to Christ. His mother had died long before that, believing she had failed.

It is my firm conviction, mother, that if you bring up your child in the discipline and instruction of the Lord, you won't fail. It may look like failure to the world. It may look like failure to you, and you may die as a seeming failure. But you can be sure of one thing: If you brought him up in the training and admonition of the Lord, God will get him; but he must have a godly mother. God had to have Jochebed to get Moses; God had to have the mother of John Newton to reach thousands. I'm sure God is looking for mothers like these in our day.

Whether or not you had a godly mother, today God Himself is calling you, friend, because He has a mother-love for you. In fact, He loves you even more than a mother loves her child. Let's not lose sight of the fact that God is the One who made mothers and can put His love in their hearts. Mother, He's the One who can make you the kind of person He wants you to be so that you can set forth the kind of God He is.

there are Judas, Demas, and Ananias and Sapphira. These are characters who walk in the shadows.

One of these, Balaam, is clearly a prophet for profit. He is one of those enigmatic and mysterious characters in the Word of God, one of the strangest characters in all of Scripture. The question arises: Is Balaam a genuine prophet of God? Or is he a religious racketeer? It's difficult to answer. Is Balaam sincerely seeking to serve God, or is he a fake, as phony as a three-dollar bill?

You be the judge. I'll attempt to tell you all that I have gathered concerning him, and I've read everything that I could put my hands on.

I will let you decide concerning this man. I'm confident that a great many people, when they read Numbers 22, 23, 24 and 25, are ready to dismiss Balaam as an unsavory and an unworthy character not worth further consideration. But you can't do that. Even before you finish the Old Testament, Micah tells us that we're to remember him. Notice what the prophet says,

O My people, remember now what Balak king of Moab counseled, and what Balaam the son of Beor answered him, from Acacia Grove to Gilgal, that you may know the righteousness of the LORD.
(Micah 6:5)

In other words, Micah says you can't forget him; you can't ignore him because he is a tremendous lesson for God's people. And the very interesting thing is that there is more said in Scripture concerning Balaam

— 3 —

BALAAM
A Prophet for Profit
Numbers 22–25

Across the pages of Scripture march men and women from all walks of life. The Holy Spirit customarily gives a camera-sharp picture of each one of them. There is generally a clear delineation of character that the Holy Spirit gives to us in a few words.

There are some exceptions to this. There are those whose character is fuzzy. Darkness hides their true nature, and we are not always sure that we have a correct estimation of it. Let me mention some of them. In the Old Testament we see Cain, Esau, Balaam, Samson, Saul, and Absalom. We can't be sure about these men. And in the New Testament there is the rich young ruler (we wonder if he ever came back to Christ);

than there is said about Mary the mother of Jesus.
There is more said about him than about ten of the
apostles of the Lord all put together. Therefore, the
Word of God does give some emphasis to him.

The New Testament mentions him three times—
always in connection with apostasy. In three of the
apocalyptic messages of the New Testament you will
find references to this man. The first is found in 2
Peter 2:15:

> **They have forsaken the right way and
> gone astray, following the way of Balaam
> the son of Beor, who loved the wages of
> unrighteousness.**

That's the first statement, a warning concerning the
"way of Balaam." And then Jude, in his little book, in
the eleventh verse, says:

> **Woe to them! For they have gone in the
> way of Cain, have run greedily in the
> error of Balaam for profit, and perished in
> the rebellion of Korah.**

Jude warns of the "error of Balaam." The *error* of
Balaam and the *way* of Balaam are not the same. Also
John in Revelation, when giving the prophetic history
of the church, traces the period when the martyr
church would stand against the world, then later when
the world like a flood would come inside the church.
Our Lord's message to that church is in Revelation
2:14:

But I have a few things against you, because you have there those who hold the doctrine of Balaam, who taught Balak to put a stumbling block before the children of Israel, to eat things sacrificed to idols, and to commit sexual immorality.

Here we are told about the "doctrine of Balaam." The *doctrine* of Balaam is different from the *way* of Balaam, and it's different from the *error* of Balaam. Therefore, in attempting to evaluate this man we need to recognize that these three statements give us a character analysis of Balaam. Let's now go back into his history, back into the Book of Numbers, to understand these warnings.

As Israel advanced toward the promised land, coming to the end of the forty years of wandering in the wilderness, they entered a new territory. It was the territory of certain nations that were their natural enemies. Israel had gained a victory as they came up against the Amorites. Naturally that word had spread so that these nations feared Israel. And when Israel came into the territory of Moab, Balak the king of Moab was afraid to engage them in battle. He resorted to a superstition; that is, he engaged a famous prophet of that day to come and curse Israel. The one he engaged is the one in whom we're interested: Balaam the prophet.

A REPUTATION FOR RESULTS

Balaam was a Midianite. He was brought from Aram, out of the mountains of the east. I should say this concerning him: Balaam uttered several of the most wonderful prophecies you'll find in the Word of God. Probably it was on the basis of his prophecy that the wise men came out of the East to Jerusalem asking the question, "Where is He that is born King of the Jews?" So, you see, we cannot dismiss this man and say we need pay no attention to him at all when he gave such an important prophecy as that. Apparently he was a prophet with a very wide reputation in that day— because he got results. And the question is: Was this man a genuine prophet of God?

Let's look at his story beginning in Numbers 22. When the children of Israel came to the east bank of the Jordan River in preparing to cross over into the land God had promised them, naturally Balak the king of Moab did not know their intentions. He did not know but what they intended to attack him and wrest his kingdom from him. Therefore, afraid to make an attack upon them but wanting to defend his kingdom, he sent messengers to Balaam. The word that he sent with the messengers was this:

Therefore please come at once, curse this people for me, for they are too mighty for me. Perhaps I shall be able to defeat them and drive them out of the land, for I know that he whom you bless is blessed, and he whom you curse is cursed.
(Numbers 22:6)

Now that reveals the reputation Balaam had. Balak sent messengers to him who stated their mission, and they brought with them a very handsome price.

So the elders of Moab and the elders of Midian departed with the diviner's fee in their hand, and they came to Balaam and spoke to him the words of Balak.
(Numbers 22:7)

They came to Balaam with a very handsome price for his services, and they said to him, "Balak has sent us, and he wants to engage your services. He wants you to curse these people that have recently come up out of Egypt. He has found that they're a dangerous people. So far they have had victories everywhere they have met the enemy, and he'd like for you to come up." Well, the very interesting thing is that this man Balaam sounds very genuine at first:

And he said to them, "Lodge here tonight, and I will bring back word to you, as the LORD speaks to me." So the princes of Moab stayed with Balaam.
(Numbers 22:8)

Have you ever heard anything more pious than that? He sounds genuine, does he not? Balaam seems to be trying honestly to ascertain the mind of God here. He said, "If you'll stay here this night, I'll make inquiry of God and see whether I'm to go with you or not." Well, he did. And he got God's answer.

And God said to Balaam, "You shall not go with them; you shall not curse the people, for they are blessed."
(Numbers 22:12)

That's God's final word to Balaam. "You're not to go, and you're not to curse these people because I have blessed them." That is God's answer. Now what will be the reaction of Balaam to that? Here is where, I must confess, I'm taken off guard.

So Balaam rose in the morning and said to the princes of Balak, "Go back to your land, for the LORD has refused to give me permission to go with you."
(Numbers 22:13)

He says, "I can't go. God has forbidden me to go. I won't go. You can return to your master and tell him."

And the princes of Moab rose and went to Balak, and said, "Balaam refuses to come with us."
(Numbers 22:14)

Now if the story ended there, I would have to say that Balaam is one of the most remarkable men of God I've ever met. Here's a man who has a prophecy from God. God gives him a message, and this man obeys the message. He says, "No, I won't go." But, unfortunately, the story does not end there.

Sometimes we also acquit ourselves in a very fine way, don't we? And it's afterward that we have our difficulty.

Now will you notice that Balak is not going to take no for an answer. And, candidly, I believe that he knew something about the character of this man Balaam.

> **Then Balak again sent princes, more numerous and more honorable than they.**
> (Numbers 22:15)

It is quite flattering that he now sends some of the most important men of the kingdom to the prophet.

> **And they came to Balaam and said to him, "Thus says Balak the son of Zippor: 'Please let nothing hinder you from coming to me; for I will certainly honor you greatly, and I will do whatever you say to me. Therefore please come, curse this people for me.'"**
> (Numbers 22:16–17)

They make him an attractive offer.

If I may use the common jargon of the street, Balak upped the ante. He decided to offer Balaam more. Apparently he knew something about character. And now listen to this pious prophet.

> **Then Balaam answered and said to the servants of Balak, "Though Balak were to give me his house full of silver and gold, I could not go beyond the word of the LORD my God, to do less or more."**
> (Numbers 22:18)

Why did he say "If he would give me a house full of silver and gold"? Because that's what he wanted. Why mention it if you're not thinking about it? "Why," he says, "I wouldn't go even if he gave me a house filled

with gold and silver." And when he makes this statement I can hear a lot of the brethren saying, "Amen.
Hallelujah for Balaam. What a testimony he's giving!"
But he's not genuine here. He's not telling the truth
here. He's going to take a little less than a house filled
with gold and silver, but it's going to be a good price.
May I say to you, he said this because he was a covetous
man. Now listen to him:

> **Now therefore, please, you also stay here
> tonight, that I may know what more the
> LORD will say to me.**
> (Numbers 22:19)

Why did he say that? He already has God's answer.
Why does he say, "Wait here tonight, and I'll go to God
again to see if He has changed His mind"? God had said
to him, "I don't want you to go, and you're positively
not to curse these people." That's God's answer. That
should have been enough. But when you begin to talk
about a house filled with silver and gold, it's well to go
back and make inquiry again. God may have changed
His mind.

You may have heard the whimsical story of the
preacher who came to his wife and said, "I've just gotten a call to the church in the next town. It's a larger
town. It's a much better church. The people in it are
more refined and cultured, and they do not cause the
trouble they do here; and they've offered me a higher
salary. I'm going upstairs and pray about this to see if
it's the Lord's will for me to go." His wife says, "Fine,
I'll go up and pray with you." And he says, "Oh, my, no.

You stay down here and pack up." Balaam, you see, is going to pray about it some more although he actually has God's answer.

However, it does look like God changes His mind, does it not? Notice the development here, for it's so important.

> **And God came to Balaam at night and said to him, "If the men come to call you, rise and go with them; but only the word which I speak to you—that you shall do."** (Numbers 22:20)

Now somebody says, "God did change His mind." No, God didn't. Some hold that there is what is known as the permissive will of God. There is also the direct will of God. And there are a great many Christians today who are taking God's second best or God's third best because they will not accept the will of God for their lives. And God permits this. Balaam already had God's mind. He didn't need to make further inquiry. But there's one thing sure—a house full of silver and gold is a nice price for a prophet, and to him there seemed to be no adequate reason why he shouldn't go. So God permitted him to go.

Perhaps, you remember that the children of Israel complained to Moses and murmured in the wilderness, "We want something besides manna to eat. We're tired of it. We want meat." And God said, "I'll give them flesh. I'll give them flesh till it comes out of their nostrils and they are sick of it." Later on, the psalmist wrote, "And He gave them their request, but sent lean-ness into their soul" (Psalm 106:15).

There are certain things that you can keep nagging God about that He'll permit you to do. But, my friend, you'll dry up spiritually. And there are a great many Christians who could testify to this experience. Do you want God's permissive will, or do you want His direct will? Do you want Him to give you every one of your prayer requests, or do you really want Him to have His way? Do you want His will to be done, or do you really want God to come over on your side and do what you want done? The interesting thing is that there are times when He will do just that.

Now this man Balaam is being permitted to go, but God is going to warn him every step of the way. And He uses something quite interesting.

So Balaam rose in the morning, saddled his donkey, and went with the princes of Moab. Then God's anger was aroused because he went, and the Angel of the Lord took His stand in the way. . . .
(Numbers 22:21–22)

The reason Balaam can't see the angel of the Lord is because he is thinking of a house full of silver and gold. He's a covetous man, and he can't see spiritual things. And you talk about a rebuke! God knows how to rebuke. This dumb animal on which he's riding sees the angel—it has more spiritual discernment than he does. Years ago some wag sent me this on a little card (I don't think he meant anything personal, but he did send it to me): "It was a miracle in Balaam's day for an ass to speak. It's a miracle today when one keeps quiet." My beloved, this is the way of Balaam. Will you listen to Peter again as he evaluates this man:

They have forsaken the right way and gone astray, following the way of Balaam the son of Beor, who loved the wages of unrighteousness.
(2 Peter 2:15)

The minute that prophet left and went with the messengers of Balak he was going astray. He was out of the will of God. He loved the wages of unrighteousness. He was covetous. Listen to Peter in the next verse:

But he was rebuked for his iniquity: a dumb donkey speaking with a man's voice restrained the madness of the prophet.

Balaam was thinking, *I just can't wait to get over there and get the job done and get my money.*

My beloved, may I speak very candidly. There are many Christian organizations today that need to be investigated. The way you measure a Christian organization is whether or not it is after the dollar. That's the way. And some of them won't stand inspection. Some of the most covetous people I've ever met are in the Lord's work. I've been in this work nearly half a century, and I've met a great many people. May I say to you, friend, it's always well to investigate and see who's getting rich.

Religion can be a racket. And I think every believer is responsible for knowing what he is supporting.

PROBING HIS PERSONALITY

Old Balaam had a message from God, but he was covetous. We're merely on the surface; now let's probe a little deeper. Let's look at the personality of Balaam. Jude tells us this:

> **Woe to them! For they have gone in the way of Cain, have run greedily in the error of Balaam for profit, and perished in the rebellion of Korah.**
> (Jude 11)

Suppose you met him and said to him, "Now, Brother Balaam, why are you going with these messengers? We understand that God has told you not to go. Why are you going?" Then he would have started rationalizing—he could have explained his actions and ascribed a worthy motive for his conduct.

The interesting thing is that there is more pious rationalization today in Christian circles than you can imagine. You and I need to examine our motives, friend. This fellow Balaam worries us, doesn't he? Here is a man with God's message, but he is rationalizing behind a very pious front.

Look at the scene in the land of Moab. Israel is camping in the valley surrounded by mountains on every side, and the king of the Moabites, Balak, brings Balaam to a mountaintop overlooking the camp. (I do not think that the Israelites knew what was taking place up there.) And Balak says, "Look! There are the people I'm talking about. I want you to curse them." Notice Balaam's answer:

> **How shall I curse whom God has not cursed? And how shall I denounce whom the LORD has not denounced? For from the top of the rocks I see him, and from the hills I behold him; There! A people dwelling alone, not reckoning itself among the nations.**
> (Numbers 23:8–9)

This is one of the greatest prophecies concerning the nation Israel, and it's given through a man who's so covetous he can't see anything but the gold and silver! Balak is dissatisfied, naturally, and he says, "You didn't curse them; you blessed them! Let's go to another mountain peak." He takes him around on another side. They go to the top of the mountain and he says, "Now take a look at them and see if you can curse them." Now hear Balaam:

> **Behold, I have received a command to bless; He has blessed and I cannot reverse it. He has not observed iniquity in Jacob, nor has He seen wickedness in Israel. The LORD his God is with him, and the shout of a King is among them.**
> (Numbers 23:20–21)

"I cannot curse them because God does not behold iniquity in Israel." Now how is he rationalizing?

Balaam reasoned that God must condemn Israel. Why? Because there was evil in the camp; there was sin in the camp. In other portions we read that there had been rebellion, there had been overt sin, and God had to judge His own people. But, my beloved, will you hear me very carefully. God will deal with His own people, but He's not going to let a heathen prophet bring an accusation against them. Whom the Lord has justified no man can condemn. And I say that is wonderful!

The natural man always concludes that God must judge Israel and judge sinners. That's natural. I've heard this a dozen times. Years ago a vile speaking man said to me after a Thursday night Bible study, "How can you say that David is a man after God's own heart when he's a murderer and an adulterer?" I said, "It is difficult, isn't it? But, brother, it sure ought to encourage you and me. If God will take David, maybe He'll take you and maybe He'll take me."

The natural man knows nothing about imputed righteousness. He knows nothing about the righteousness that God makes over to a condemned sinner when he receives Christ—because Christ died for him on the cross, and He was raised from the dead. Now that sinner is put in Christ, and God sees him in Christ. Paul says:

What then shall we say to these things? If God is for us, who can be against us? He who did not spare His own Son, but delivered Him up for us all, how shall He not with Him also freely give us all things?

Who shall bring a charge against God's elect? It is God who justifies.
(Romans 8:31–33)

Who shall bring a charge against God's elect? Old Balaam could not—nor can any person today or even Satan bring a charge against a sinner who has turned to Jesus Christ.

Who is he who condemns? It is Christ who died, and furthermore is also risen, who is even at the right hand of God, who also makes intercession for us.
(Romans 8:34)

This very day when Satan, the accuser of the brethren, presents himself before God and accuses one who belongs to Christ, the Lord Jesus Christ becomes the believer's advocate. He says to the Father, "I died for him. He is in Me. And You can receive him just as You receive Me." Balaam doesn't know anything about that. That's the error of Balaam. And that's the error of a great many folk today.

HIS DEMONIC DOCTRINES

Let's probe a little deeper now by going into the thought life of Balaam. This brings us to his doctrine. The doctrine of Balaam is satanic, it is demonic, it is hellish, and it is subtle. It's the same thing that appeared in the Garden of Eden to our first parents. In our Lord's message to the church at Pergamum He said:

But I have a few things against you, because you have there those who hold the doctrine of Balaam, who taught Balak to put a stumbling block before the children of Israel, to eat things sacrificed to idols, and to commit sexual immorality. (Revelation 2:14)

Balaam, you see, finds that God will not permit him to curse these people. He realizes he would have to adopt a different approach if he's going to get the silver and gold—and that's what he has come for, after all. If you think Balaam is going back empty-handed, you are not acquainted with religious racketeers. Because he wants the rich gifts of Balak, he's going to do something now that's terrible.

Now Israel remained in Acacia Grove, and the people began to commit harlotry with the women of Moab. (Numbers 25:1)

As you read this awful account that follows, you will see what happened as a result of Balaam's counsel. He says something like this to Balak, "Now I can't curse them, but I can tell you how to destroy them. You go down and join them—get the good-looking women of Moab to go down to the camp and get acquainted." And so the Moabite women "caused the children of Israel, through the counsel of Balaam, to trespass against the LORD . . ." (Numbers 31:16). With fornication came idolatry into the camp of Israel. What the devil couldn't do hy cursing and fighting from the outside, he did from the inside.

Do you know that the church has never been hurt from the outside? The finest years of the church were during its persecution. Never has the church been as rich spiritually, never has it been as evangelistic, never has it reached out to the ends of the earth as it did during those periods. The devil was fighting it from the outside. But he caught on. He couldn't hurt the church from the outside, so he joined it. Read the story of Constantine. Read about the entrance of all sorts of pagan rituals and rites that were incorporated from the inside. What Satan couldn't do from the outside he did from within. There's a great principle here that is applicable to all relationships. Our country, for example, will not, in my opinion, be hurt as a nation from the outside. But I do think we're being destroyed from the inside. At the present time it is also happening to a church I could name. There is not an enemy on the outside that has ever hurt that church, but I know some members who have. A church can be crucified from the inside. That's a principle which Satan has learned.

Let me now make a personal application. Do we understand how God justifies a sinner? Can we say with Paul that there is now no condemnation to them who are in Christ Jesus? The death and resurrection of Christ are my hope today; and because these constitute my hope, I stand before God with no condemnation. But that doesn't end the story.

You and I need to search our own motives, our motives for conduct and action. Why really do you attend church? What is the motive behind your service in the church? Are you seeking applause? Are you seeking power? Perhaps wealth? What's your motive? The difficulty with many of us today is we're acting from mixed motives, and there's frustration in our lives. We're rather like old Balaam. Have you decided whether he's really God's man or not? What kind of fellow is this who could give these wonderful prophecies of God and talk about his relationship to God and then do the thing that he did? He was acting from mixed motives, to say the least. Oh, there are so many today who say, "I want to be a Christian, but I want to go just as far into the world as I can."

Although I don't like to close with this kind of story, I will do so because it illustrates my point. The teacher in a class of little boys had given them the story of Lazarus and the rich man. She told about the plight of Lazarus, the beggar. She told about how he suffered down here and what he went through. My, she painted it black. Then she told about the rich man and what he enjoyed in this life. Then she moved over on the other side and told about where the rich man went after death—he went to hades. She told about the poor man who was in Abraham's bosom. That class of little boys was quite solemn. In order to clinch it, she asked, "Which would you rather be, the rich man or Lazarus the beggar?" Well, not one of those little fellows answered. She waited a few moments for it to sink in. Finally, one little fellow put up his hand. He said, "I'd like to be the rich man here and Lazarus hereafter."

There are a lot of Christians like that today. They want to be the rich man here and Lazarus over there—and they think they can do it. If Balaam is in heaven, then they can do it. But the Holy Spirit doesn't even tell us. You figure it out.

And then I read further on that Balaam was killed by the Israelites (Numbers 31:8). He was on the wrong side—Balaam, a prophet for profit. What kind of man was he? What kind of Christian are you today? What kind of Christian am I? Paul says that we ought to examine ourselves. If you are God's child, you are not under condemnation before Him, and He won't accept Satan's charge against you. But He Himself will search your heart and He will search mine.

— 4 —

MICAIAH
A God-Aimed Arrow
1 Kings 22

There is the ever-present temptation when we come to the record given in 1 and 2 Kings to emphasize some phase of the life of Elijah. He dominates this era, and his life is rich in interest and in spiritual content. However, there is another prophet who is as little-known as Elijah is well-known. You may not be acquainted with him at all. I want to say this for him: He's in the major league with Elijah. Although he may not be as well-known as Elijah, he hit just as many home runs for God as Elijah did.

The difficulty with the prophet we are looking at is that every time he preached a sermon he was put in jail! The reason they put him in jail is that he happened to be the one man standing for God in the courts of

Ahab, and what he said was always unfavorable to Ahab. As you know, a great many people do not like to have anything said that is unfavorable to them, and that was true of Ahab, king of Israel.

You will recall in the history of Israel the glorious reign of Solomon; but it concluded with the warning given to him that the kingdom was to be divided. Well, it *was* divided and there were ten tribes in the north and the one tribe, Judah (with little Benjamin), in the south. Israel and Judah were to walk their separate ways, but both were to go finally into captivity.

The very interesting thing is that at this particular moment in history we have Ahab, the king of Israel, in the north. He's the worst king they ever had—probably the worst king that any kingdom ever had. In contrast, we have in the south Jehoshaphat, king of Judah; and he is one of the very best kings they ever had. Normally these two kingdoms would have been farther apart than they ever were in their history, but at this time they were more closely allied. It was an abnormal alliance; it was an unnatural confederacy. The fraternizing of these two kings who were mutual antipathies seemed strange indeed.

The explanation is not difficult to find. Right down beneath the surface you find that Jehoram, son of Jehoshaphat, king of Judah, had married Athaliah, the daughter of Ahab, king of Israel. (She was to become known as the bloody Athaliah after she killed her grandchildren.) Here is a case when again the sons of God and the daughters of men had intermarried, and of course it wrought havoc. (We see the first occurence of this in Genesis 6.) It always will bring havoc, at any time, under any dispensation, at any period in the history of this world, when the sons of God marry the daughters of men—that is, when the saved marry the unsaved.

Now these two men, Ahab and Jehoshaphat, are far apart in their thinking and in their relationship to God, yet you find them joining up.

Ahab had invited Jehoshaphat over for a visit. They're kinfolk now anyway, so it was natural to get together for a visit. And while Jehoshaphat was there Ahab evidently had planned to say at a particular moment, "We have lost Ramoth Gilead to the king of Syria. It's necessary for us to go and get it, and I'm just wondering, Jehoshaphat, if you'd like to join with me in going and rescuing this part of our nation. Would you join with me?" Lo and behold, Jehoshaphat agrees to it. He says, "Yes, I would be perfectly willing to join with you."

Now this man Jehoshaphat was God's man. As we see in the Book of Chronicles, one of the five revival periods took place during his reign. He had a heart for God, and he wanted to do the will of God, which is evident in the request he makes:

Also Jehoshaphat said to the king of Israel, "Please inquire for the word of the LORD today."
(1 Kings 22:5)

In other words, he said, "I'll be glad to join with you, but I want to know what God's will is in the matter. I'm wondering if you would bring the prophets in, and let's find out what the will of God is."

So this man Ahab had trotted in the paid preachers of the day.

> **Then the king of Israel gathered the prophets together, about four hundred men, and said to them, "Shall I go against Ramoth Gilead to fight, or shall I refrain?" So they said, "Go up, for the LORD will deliver it into the hand of the king."**
> (1 Kings 22:6)

They are saying, you see, the thing that Ahab wanted to hear.

This has always been a great danger and is the place to which the pulpit in America has come. Someone has said that the pulpit in America has become a sounding board instead of the voice in the wilderness crying out for God. It is saying the thing that people want to hear today. That is the tragedy of this hour in which we live.

These prophets who all eat at the table of Ahab know which side their bread is buttered on, and so they say the thing that Ahab wants to hear. They say, "Go on up to battle; you'll win."

Now this man Jehoshaphat is God's man, and he has spiritual discernment. He knows that these four hundred prophets are not giving God's message.

> **And Jehoshaphat said, "Is there not still a prophet of the LORD here, that we may inquire of Him?"**
> (1 Kings 22:7)

Jehoshaphat is wondering, "Couldn't we get a really spiritually minded prophet that has the mind of the Lord and has the courage to declare it? Don't you have a man like that?"

> **So the king of Israel said unto Jehoshaphat, "There is still one man, Micaiah the son of Imlah, by whom we may inquire of the LORD . . .**
> (1 Kings 22:8)

Thank God for the one man, but what a tragic hour— "There is yet *one* man." There are four hundred men who are willing to please the king and *one* man willing to stand for God, and he names him; he is Micaiah.

Now here is his introduction. The kings have had dinner together, you remember, and now Ahab is introducing, as it were, their after-dinner speaker. How would you like an introduction like this: "But I hate him . . . " Ahab said, "Yes, there is one prophet here in the kingdom who speaks for the Lord, but I hate him." And I tell you, the man who gives God's Word will come in under the lash, the tongue-lashing, of those who do not want the Word of God today.

> **. . . I hate him, because he does not prophesy good concerning me, but evil. . . .**
> (1 Kings 22:8)

You hear some people say today, "When I go to church, I want to be comforted." I heard of a man who left a church that I was pastoring for the reason that he wasn't being comforted. If what they tell me about his business is true, he doesn't need comfort. He needs to be rebuked. May I say to you, my friends, in this hour we probably need something other than comforting words in America. Our nation has come to a place where people do not want to hear the things which have to do with sin, the things which rebuke them within. They do not want the Word of God really turned upon their souls and upon their hearts and upon their lives.

So Ahab says, "I hate him." And actually that is the best compliment that Micaiah ever had. I heard some time ago a famous preacher in America say this, "I do not judge a man by the friends that he has. I judge him by the enemies that he makes. And if he has the right enemies, he's the right kind of man." We are known today not only by the friends we keep, but also we're known by the enemies that we make. I heard of a man the other day at whose funeral service the preacher said, "This man did not have an enemy." Well, when I was told that, I said, "I did not know that Mr. Milquetoast had died." He is the only one who could die without having an enemy. The best thing that you could say for Micaiah was that Ahab hated him. If Ahab had loved him, there would have been something wrong with Micaiah.

In our day there is a notion being circulated throughout America, and it's being called Christianity, that we're to love everything and that we're to love everybody. Even the secular press has had to call attention to the fact that America has lost its moral consciousness. Even the church has lost its conscience in America today and has no moral courage whatsoever.

I love this fellow Micaiah. In this day of compromise it is wonderful to see a man like this. In a day when it's peace at any price, in a day when men are compromising in every field—especially in politics and religion—it's wonderful to see this man stand out for God. And this is the man we're considering now, this forgotten prophet, Micaiah, who apparently spent most of his active ministry in jail. He would come out and give a message, and back to jail he would go. And that's where he was when he was summoned to appear before Ahab and Jehoshaphat.

Actually, Micaiah was the best friend Ahab ever had. If he had only listened to Micaiah, his life would have been spared; he would not have been killed in battle. But he did not listen. It reminds me of what Paul said to the Galatians: "Have I therefore become your enemy because I tell you the truth?" (Galatians 4:16).

Now will you notice this dramatic scene that is before us. To me this is one of the richest scenes you will find in the Word of God.

The king of Israel and Jehoshaphat the king of Judah, having put on their robes, sat each on his throne, at a threshing floor at the entrance of the gate of Samaria; and all the prophets prophesied before them.
(1 Kings 22:10)

Here are these two sovereigns. One sits upon the throne of Judah, and the other sits upon the throne of Israel. Before them are four hundred prophets—the boys who are paid to say the nice things—going around smiling and saying to Ahab, "Go up, go up. You will win the battle. Everything will be in your favor. You go right ahead and do this." That's the scene.

Jehoshaphat, however, is puzzled. He is not satisfied with what these paid preachers are saying. A guard is sent over now to get Micaiah who is in jail. They keep him handy; they always know where he is when they *do* want a word from God.

On the way back the messenger says to him, "Now look here, Micaiah, you're just a killjoy here at this court; and you never say anything that puts you in good standing with Ahab. I want to suggest to you that you go ahead and agree with the prophets. They've all told the king to go against Ramoth Gilead and that God would give it to him. If you'll just join in the chorus there loud and lustily, it will put you in favor, and we won't have to bring you back to jail again." Listen to Micaiah:

And Micaiah said, "As the Lord lives, whatever the Lord says to me, that I will speak."
(1 Kings 22:14)

Micaiah comes in now. These four hundred prophets are milling around, the two kings are sitting on their thrones, Jehoshaphat is a little puzzled, and Ahab says:

. . . Micaiah, shall we go to war against Ramoth Gilead, or shall we refrain? . . .
(1 Kings 22:15)

Now here is a man with a sense of humor. God has a sense of humor, friend, and His Word is filled with it. Here is an example. Micaiah looks about and sees what is going on so he mimics the prophets.

> **. . . And he answered him, "Go and pros-
> per, for the LORD will deliver it into the
> hand of the king!"**
> (1 Kings 22:15)

And I think he begins to trot around with the other prophets.

Ahab knows this fellow, and he knows he is pulling his leg. He knows he has not yet given the message from God.

> **So the king said to him, "How many times
> shall I make you swear that you tell me
> nothing but the truth in the name of the
> LORD?"**
> (1 Kings 22:16)

"Quit kidding me, Micaiah. What is the message?"

Now Micaiah becomes serious, and he gives God's message. Listen to it:

> **Then he said, "I saw all Israel scattered on
> the mountains, as sheep that have no
> shepherd. And the LORD said, 'These have
> no master. Let each return to his house in
> peace.'"**
> (1 Kings 22:17)

It means that Ahab will be killed in battle. He, of course, is the master of his people. You would think that Ahab would receive this message and thank the prophet for giving him a word that would have spared his life. He should have been grateful to him. But notice his reaction:

And the king of Israel said to Jehoshaphat, "Did I not tell you he would not prophesy good concerning me, but evil?"
(1 Kings 22:18)

"He never says anything good to me. He always says things that are bad about me, and I don't like it. I hate him!" That's Ahab. Micaiah was the only one there who *did* know the truth and the only one there giving the truth.

Now the prophet does something that is, without doubt, one of the most masterly things you'll find in the entire Word of God. It was a dramatic scene before, but it becomes doubly dramatic now. This man Micaiah uses satire, biting satire. He uses the rapier of ridicule, and it's devastating. Listen to him as he gives this word that all Israel is to be scattered and Ahab is to be killed. Poor old Ahab has just said, "I told you so. That's the thing he always says—bad news for me." Then Micaiah gives a parable. (You remember that our Lord turned to parables only when the people would not hear. Parables are for folk who will not hear God's Word. It is the way to elicit their interest and at least get the message to them.)

HIS WORD IS TRUE

Micaiah gives a preposterous parable; it's one of these parables by contrast. As you know, a parable is given to illustrate truth. In fact, the word *parable* is in the Greek *balo*, meaning "to throw," and *para*, meaning "by the side of." It means to throw or put down by the side of a thing something else to measure it. If you put a yardstick down beside the desk in front of me, that's a parable. It tells you how long it is. And so a parable is something that is put down by the side of something else to illustrate it. But at times it illustrates by contrast. The Lord Jesus gave parables like that. When the religious rulers began to turn from Him, He gave the parable of the unjust judge. He said that there was a widow who camped on his doorstep, and the unjust judge did not want to hear her case because she had no political power nor did she carry any vote in his community. But she stayed there and stayed there and stayed there some more until he had to hear her to get rid of her. Now do you think that God is an unjust judge and that you have to camp on His doorstep, that you have to plead and beg Him to do something for you? No. He is the opposite. It is a parable by contrast, you see.

Now notice the parable that Micaiah gives. I wish I could have seen this Jew as he gave it. I'm confident there was a gleam in his eye and a wry smile on his face. Here it is:

Then Micaiah said, "Therefore hear the word of the LORD: I saw the LORD sitting on His throne, and all the host of heaven standing by, on His right hand and on His left."
(1 Kings 22:19)

In other words, there is a special "board of directors" meeting called in heaven, with God as the chairman of the board.

> **And the Lord said, "Who will persuade Ahab to go up, that he may fall at Ramoth Gilead?" So one spoke in this manner, and another spoke in that manner.**
> (1 Kings 22:20)

Isn't that ridiculous? Imagine God calling a meeting of the board of directors in heaven and saying, "Now I've called you together in order to get some advice. A problem has come up that is too big for Me to handle. Ahab is to go to battle and be killed, but how in the world will I get him into battle? I just don't know what to do." And one spirit got up and said, "I think this." And the rest shook their heads and said, "No, that doesn't sound good." Another spirit got up and said something else. Everybody shook their heads and said, "No, that won't do either." Finally one little spirit got up with a suggestion that sounded like a good one. (I wish I had been there to ask Micaiah how a spirit stands!) But he was smiling all the time he was saying this, you see. I like the way Micaiah tells it:

> **Then a spirit came forward and stood before the Lord, and said, "I will persuade him."**
> (1 Kings 22:21)

My friend, can you imagine God asking for advice? It is utterly ridiculous. Notice Isaiah 40:13; "Who has directed the Spirit of the LORD, or as His counselor has taught Him?" God hasn't been to school; no one has taught Him. God never asks anybody for advice. The apostle Paul exclaimed in Romans 11:33–34:

Oh, the depth of the riches both of the wisdom and knowledge of God! How unsearchable are His judgments and His ways past finding out! For who has known the mind of the LORD? Or who has become His counselor?

Have you noticed that when our Lord Jesus Christ was down here in the flesh there were two things He never did? He never did appeal to His own mind as being the final place of decision for any action that He took. He never said to anyone, "I'm going to do this because I've been thinking about it all night and I've come to the conclusion it's the best thing to do." Every time He did something He said, "This is My Father's will. I've come to do My Father's will." He never appealed to His own mind even when He was a man. And then the second thing: He never asked anybody for advice. He never called together His disciples and said, "Now, fellows, I'm in a quandary. Shall I go to Jerusalem or shall I stay here?" Never did He ask them that. There was one exception, I grant you, at the feeding of the 5,000. He turned to Philip and asked, "Where shall we buy bread?" But the Gospel writer hastens to add, "But this He said to test him, for He Himself knew what He would do" (John 6:6). The Lord Jesus never asked anybody for advice.

Oh, today, my friend, God is not asking for advice; down here He doesn't need our advice. How many fine Christian organizations and movements that were started by godly men, led of God, have fallen into the hands of unspiritual men who are determined to have their way and are riding roughshod over the hearts and lives of multitudes? Oh, my friend, your way is not better than God's way! God does not want your advice. He is not asking how to run His business. He is telling you and me what to do. God does not need advice!

However, Micaiah imagines Him in a board of directors meeting where God is puzzled and is getting information. Now Micaiah makes his point:

> **Then a spirit came forward and stood before the LORD, and said, "I will persuade him." The LORD said to him, "In what way?" So he said, "I will go out and be a lying spirit in the mouth of all his prophets." And the LORD said, "You shall persuade him, and also prevail. Go out and do so." Therefore, look! The LORD has put a lying spirit in the mouth of all these prophets of yours, and the LORD has declared disaster against you.**
> (1 Kings 22:21–23)

This is sparkling, striking, and startling satire. I do not know of a better way of calling the crowd of prophets there a bunch of liars than to tell this little story. That's exactly what Micaiah is doing. He says that this spirit came from God as a lying spirit in the mouth of these false prophets.

Now Ahab doesn't like it, of course. He wants to get rid of Micaiah.

So the king of Israel said, "Take Micaiah, and return him to Amon the governor of the city and to Joash the king's son; and say, 'Thus says the king: "Put this fellow in prison, and feed him with bread of affliction and water of affliction, until I come in peace."'"
(1 Kings 22:26–27)

In other words, "Wait until I get back from the battle. I'll take care of him for talking to me like that!" But Micaiah had the last word:

But Micaiah said, "If you ever return in peace, the LORD has not spoken by me." And he said, "Take heed, all you people!"
(1 Kings 22:28)

In effect he said, "Listen. If you even come back here, Ahab, the Lord hasn't spoken by me. And I don't care about your hearing it because you're not coming back, but I want these other people to hear it so they will know I was speaking God's word to you."

Well, the armies of Ahab and Jehoshaphat went to battle against the king of Syria. This man Ahab has a bag filled with tricks. He has persuaded Jehoshaphat to go into the battle on his side; and knowing the king of Syria is after him, Ahab says to Jehoshaphat, "You keep on your king's robes, but I'll change into a regular buck private's outfit." And he does that. It is a perfect disguise. There is not a way in the world for the king of Syria to know who Ahab is. The battle is joined and, I tell you, it is fortunate that Jehoshaphat is not killed in battle. He is almost taken, but he escapes by the skin of his teeth, and he returns like a whipped dog licking his wounds.

For awhile it looks as if Ahab will escape like the slippery eel that he is. It looks as if Providence is on his side, that the prophecy is wrong and Micaiah is to be confused and God mocked. But then something happens.

One fellow in the infantry of the enemy, equipped with bow and arrows, has one arrow left. *Well,* he thinks, *no use keeping it. I want my sergeant to think I was busy shooting the Israelites so I'll get rid of this one.* The record puts it this way:

Now a certain man drew a bow at random. . . .
(1 Kings 22:34)

He just pulled it. He didn't aim at Ahab. King Ahab had on a regular soldier's uniform; nobody knew who he was. And this soldier just pulls his bow at random and lets the arrow fly. But that arrow has Ahab's name on it, and God had written it there.

My friend, we've heard a great deal about guided missiles in our day. This is a guided missile, and probably the first one. God was guiding this missile, and it reached its destination. It was a God-aimed arrow, and it found its way between the joints of the armor of Ahab and found its way to his heart. He was mortally wounded. He told his charioteer to take him out of battle, that he had been hit.

> **The battle increased that day; and the king was propped up in his chariot, facing the Syrians, and died at evening. The blood ran out from the wound onto the floor of the chariot . . . . So the king died, and was brought to Samaria. And they buried the king in Samaria. Then someone washed the chariot at a pool in Samaria, and the dogs licked up his blood while the harlots bathed, according to the word of the LORD which He had spoken.**
> (1 Kings 22:35; 37–38)

God, through Elijah, had already told Ahab this would happen because he had caused the death of Naboth so he could seize his property.

> **. . . Thus says the LORD: "In the place where dogs licked the blood of Naboth, dogs shall lick your blood, even yours."**
> (1 Kings 21:19)

So the body of the king of Israel was brought back to Samaria. And they washed the chariot of his blood and the dogs licked it, just as God said it would come to pass—literally fulfilled. Now Ahab's death probably was listed in the paper as being totally accidental, but in God's record it was providential.

And today, without any apology at all, may I say that God is still using that method. And God never misses. The psalmist says: "But God shall shoot at them with an arrow; suddenly they shall be wounded" (Psalm 64:7). There is many a man today going through this world who says, "I've escaped so far. Everything that has happened to me has been good. I do not have to answer to God." I say to you this day, there is an arrow that has already been shot from the bow in heaven with his name on it, and that arrow is the arrow of judgment when he will stand before Almighty God.

Sometimes even God's own have an arrow shot at them. You remember the thing that Job said: "For the arrows of the Almighty are within me . . ." (Job 6:4). Job found, even as God's man, that sometimes God wounds one of His own and brings him down to humble him.

But, my beloved, when the arrow of my sin was aimed, it went into Christ Jesus. Someone has said that we entered the heart of Christ through a spear wound. And the arrow of my sin wounded Him. The arrow of my sin put Him to death. Isaiah expresses it this way:

But He was wounded for our transgressions, He was bruised for our iniquities; . . . yet it pleased the LORD to bruise Him; He has put Him to grief. . . .
(Isaiah 53:5, 10)

He stepped in front of the arrow of God's judgment that was intended for you and me in order that we might never have to come into judgment. We are passed from judgment into life.

And now the psalmist says something else:

You shall not be afraid of the terror by night, nor of the arrow that flies by day.
(Psalm 91:5)

That arrow that is flying by day is the arrow that's aimed at my sin. It has already found its mark in Christ. Therefore I need not be afraid of the arrow that flies by day.

Right now your sin is either on you or it's on Christ. If you, by faith, receive Him, then He bears that sin for you. He becomes your Savior, and you will never have to come into judgment, but you are passed from death unto life. The arrows of God's judgment fell upon Him.

— 5 —

AMOS

The Country Preacher Who Came to Town
Amos 7:7–17

In the days of Amos (8th century B.C.) God's message through this remarkable prophet dealt with the fact that God's people were breaking His laws which He had given "that it may go well with you and your children after you forever" (Deuteronomy 12:28). Amos was angry at the violence they had done to the justice and the righteousness of God.

Since Amos and the little book that bears his nam⌐ may be unfamiliar to you, let me set the stage by ⌐ ing the section of Scripture that we will be look⌐ in this very interesting chapter.

Thus He showed me: Behold, the Lord stood on a wall made with a plumb line, with a plumb line in His hand.
And the LORD said to me, "Amos, what do you see?" And I said, "A plumb line." Then the Lord said:

"Behold, I am setting a plumb line
In the midst of My people Israel;
I will not pass by them anymore.
The high places of Isaac shall be desolate,
And the sanctuaries of Israel shall be laid waste.
I will rise with the sword against the house of Jeroboam."

Then Amaziah the priest of Bethel sent to Jeroboam king of Israel, saying, "Amos has conspired against you in the midst of the house of Israel. The land is not able to bear all his words.
For thus Amos has said:

'Jeroboam shall die by the sword,
And Israel shall surely be led away captive
From their own land.'"

Then Amaziah said to Amos:

"Go, you seer!
Flee to the land of Judah.
There eat bread,
And there prophesy.
But never again prophesy at Bethel,

For it is the king's sanctuary,
And it is the royal residence."

Then Amos answered, and said to Amaziah:

"I was no prophet,
Nor was I a son of a prophet,
But I was a sheepbreeder
And a tender of sycamore fruit.
Then the LORD took me as I followed the
flock,
And the LORD said to me,
'Go, prophesy to My people Israel.'
Now therefore, hear the word of the
LORD:
You say, 'Do not prophesy against Israel,
And do not spout against the house
of Isaac.'

"Therefore thus says the LORD:

'Your wife shall be a harlot in the city;
Your sons and daughters shall fall by the
sword;
Your land shall be divided by survey
line;
You shall die in a defiled land;
And Israel shall surely be led away
captive
From his own land.'"
(Amos 7:7–17)

Six miles south of Bethlehem is Tekoa. It is littl
wonder if you have never heard of it. Figurativel
is a wide spot in the road, a whistle-stop on a br

line. Today it is a ghost town. The name *Tekoa* means "a camping ground." It was not much more than that even in its heyday. It was a country place. Using the common colloquialism of the day, it was the jumping-off place. Years ago I heard a man say that to reach the place where he was born you go as far as possible by buggy, then you get off and walk two miles. That's Tekoa also.

Tekoa is the birthplace of Amos. This fact is the little town's only claim to greatness. It is true that one of David's mighty men was born there. But the thing that gives it character and notoriety is that Amos the prophet was born in Tekoa.

Now Tekoa is on the edge of a most frightful wilderness. Tekoa is situated on a ridge on the extreme edge of the inhabited area overlooking that wilderness, a wilderness that extends down to the Dead Sea, going down and down and down. You can stand there and see the Dead Sea. You can turn in the other directions and look on the other side of the ridge toward Hebron, then down into the Negev where there is more wilderness. Any way you turn you see wilderness, but the wilderness down toward the Dead Sea is the most frightful of all.

It is a desert wilderness where wild animals howl at night. By day the only thing you can see is the ground spotted by the remains of Bedouin camps—just the blackened ground left by nomads, vagabonds of the desert passing through. No one lives there. It was Dr. dam Smith who said, "The men of Tekoa looked out n a desolate and haggard world." That's the pic-You couldn't live in a worse place than Tekoa, my friend. And this was the hometown of Amos the prophet.

Amos tells us that he was a herdsman or sheep-breeder. The word that is used is an unusual word. It actually has to do with the sheep he was herding, which were a peculiar strain of sheep noted for their fine wool and bred only in the desert. They were hardy and rugged—the only kind that could live in such a place. I am told that today in that same wilderness one may see Bedouins herding that same breed of sheep.

To supplement a meager income, this man tells us something else that he did. He was a gatherer of sycamore fruit. To be more accurate, the word is *nipper*—he was a "nipper" of sycamores. The variety of sycamores that grew at a lower level in Tekoa was a kind of fig, growing on tall, heavily foliaged trees. The fruit was inferior, and because it did not ripen easily, a "nipper" treatment was adopted to hasten the ripening. That was what Amos did. He was a fruitpicker and a herdsman out there.

In other words, he really did not come from the town of Tekoa. That would have been bad enough. He came from deep in that wilderness. His sheep and his sycamores pushed him way out into that terrible desert. He was a country boy; he was a rustic; he was a hayseed. But don't let that fool you. This man Amos had the greatest world view of any of the prophets. Just because you don't like the way he dressed or where he came from, don't think he was a fool. This man had a message, an ecumenical message and a long-range point of view. Listen to him:

> **Then the LORD took me as I followed the flock, and the LORD said to me, "Go, prophesy to My people Israel."**
> (Amos 7:15)

God's seminary was in the solitude of the desert. That is where God, from the beginning, has trained His men. Remember that when God called Abraham, who was a city slicker from Ur of the Chaldees, God brought him to a wilderness near Hebron. That was a place where a man could be alone with God. It was there that Abraham raised his altar to God. The desert seems to be God's training ground.

Also, Moses was reared in a palace—educated in the greatest university of his day, the University of the Sun, which would compare favorably with our modern universities. But with all of his education and accomplishments God couldn't use him. So He sent him out to the backside of the desert of Midian and gave him a forty-year course. That is where God trained him.

David, a shepherd boy, was brought as a musician into the palace of King Saul. But God could not let him be educated there. He could not use David, grown soft from court life. God used the jealousy of the king to force him into the wild mountains and lonely caves of a wilderness existence. In such a setting God trained His king.

John the Baptist was out in the desert until his appearing to the nation. The apostle Paul, after his conversion, went into the desert of Arabia where God trained him. The apostle John was put on the Isle of

Patmos so God could give him the Book of the Revelation. Such is God's method with His men.

Out on the desert God called Amos to preach. He gave him a message, then He sent him to Bethel to give His Word to Israel.

When Amos arrived in Bethel, I think folk on the street exchanged smiles. To get this down where we live, let's say that he was wearing his first pair of hardsoled shoes. He was wearing his first necktie, and he was always loosening it because he had never worn a necktie before. But when you go up to Bethel, you must have a necktie, you know. When the pulpit committee met him, they were embarrassed. They had heard he was a great preacher, but they had not expected him to be so countrified. Everyone was embarrassed except Amos. He had come up to give God's message, and he was going to give it.

You see, Bethel was the capital of the Northern Kingdom of Israel. It was here that Jeroboam had erected one of his golden calves. This was the center of false religion. While it was the center of cults, it was also the center of culture. Bethel was sophisticated. Folk were blasé; they were uptown; they were really citified in Bethel. What was done in Bethel was the thing to do. Bethel had influence. The styles that were worn in Bethel were imitated.

The suit Amos wore was not cut according to the pattern of Bethel, and neither were his sermons cut according to the pattern of Bethel.

This man has now left the back country and has come to the boulevards. He has left the desert of Tekoa and has come to the drawing rooms of Bethel. He is out of place. He knows all about raising long-haired sheep, but he doesn't know much about these well-groomed sleek sheep to whom he is to give God's message in Bethel. He has left the place of agriculture and has come into the city of culture, Bethel. The country preacher has come to town.

Now almost everybody came to hear him at first because word had gotten around, "If you want to be entertained, go hear Amos! You ought to see the suit he's wearing—and that necktie!" They came for amusement, but they left in anger, at least most of them did. He was a sensational preacher.

Today I know a great many preachers who say they do not like sensational subjects or sensational preaching. Their criticism stems from a personal inability. The reason they don't like it is that they cannot produce it. Amos was sensational. As he preached the Word of God, people were moved. A few turned to God. Bethel was stirred.

You probably know what happened. It happened then; it happens today. Organized religion tried to silence him. The denominational leaders called a meeting. They said, "We've got to remove him. We will withdraw our support from him. Has anyone talked to him about his losing his pension if he doesn't stop this type of preaching? We do not preach this way in Bethel, and we cannot permit him to preach like that!" Even some of the fundamental leaders—"evangelicals" as they happily call themselves—were jealous and began to criticize him. They tried to undermine his ministry by circulating false reports about him. However, in spite of it all, God blessed him. Amos would not compromise. He would not shut his eyes to evil.

A mass meeting of all the false religions was called. Their motto was, "Away with Amos," and placards were carried reading "Go home, Amos! Go home!"

They decided to appoint a man to go talk to him. Amaziah, the false priest, the hired hand of idolatry, was their choice. He was, I think, one of the biggest rascals you will find on (or off) the pages of Scripture. He was an ecclesiastical politician, and these boys always move cleverly.

Now Amos is a very strong preacher. He does not mince words. He does not pull any punches. He speaks what God has instructed him to say. Listen to him in Amos 7:

> **The high places of Isaac shall be desolate, and the sanctuaries of Israel shall be laid waste. I will rise with the sword against the house of Jeroboam.**
> (v. 9)

Now watch this religious rascal, Amaziah, move:

> **Then Amaziah the priest of Bethel sent to Jeroboam king of Israel, saying, "Amos has conspired against you in the midst of the house of Israel. The land is not able to bear all his words."**
> (v. 10)

Notice his maneuver:

> **For thus Amos has said: "Jeroboam shall die by the sword. . . ."**
> (v. 11)

Let me ask you, friend, is that what Amos said? No, he had not said that. His actual words were that God had said, "I will rise with the sword against the house of Jeroboam." And if you follow the record, you will find that this pronouncement was accurate. Too bad that Jeroboam II did not believe what Amos had actually said because his grandson will be slain with the sword, and that will end his kingly line. Notice that Amos had not said that Jeroboam would perish by the sword. You see, these ecclesiastical politicians twist the truth. It is true that Amos had said something about the sword, but not that Jeroboam would die by the sword as Amaziah intentionally misquoted. Such a twisting of the truth is the worst kind of lying.

You see what Amaziah is doing—he is getting the authorities on his side before he moves in on the prophet. Though I cannot prove this, I do not think he moved alone. Such men do not move alone; they move by committees. And I think he took a committee with him. My guess is there was a committee of three, with Amaziah as chairman. Dr. Sounding Brass was on the committee. He was president of the School of the Prophets—false prophets. He was pompous and proud, an ecclesiastical politician to his fingertips. Though he himself could not preach, he was teaching other young men how to preach. Also there was Rev. Tinkling Cymbal, pastor of the wealthiest and most influential church in Bethel. He was the yes-man of the rich. He couldn't preach either, but he was a great little mixer. Oh, he was skilled at shaking hands and backslapping and attending knife and fork clubs. And if the company was right, he didn't mind taking a cocktail. His aim was to win friends. Here then is the committee that waits upon Amos: Amaziah, priest of the Golden Calf; Dr. Sounding Brass; and Rev. Tinkling Cymbal.

Oh, my friend, what a scene! Here is our prophet. He is God's man, but he does not have his hair styled, and he does not wear the correct clothes. He is country; he's from the wilderness of Tekoa. He is not accustomed to drawing rooms and committee meetings.

Here comes the committee to wait on Amos. Amaziah, the polished, cultured scholar with the rapier of ridicule and an air of condescension, addresses Amos as *seer*. What sarcasm! As you know, these ecclesiastical politicians are very polite on the surface, but, oh, they can be ugly underneath! Amaziah continues, "*Go, flee away.*" What he means is, "Get out of town! Get lost. We do not want you here anymore."

Then he makes this nasty insinuation, "Flee to the land of Judah. There eat bread, and there prophesy." In other words, "After all, Amos, you are doing this for the money. And if you go back to your hometown, you will probably be able to get good offerings there. Why don't you leave here?" What a cutting thing to say to God's man!

Then his crowning insult: "But never again prophesy at Bethel, for it is the king's sanctuary, and it is the royal residence." His satirical suggestion is, "Do you realize, Amos, that you are no preacher? Do you realize that you are speaking here at the 'First Bapterian Church,' the most prominent and influential church in the denomination? Do you know that the king attends this church? His pew is right over there. Your messages have been disturbing him. He likes to come here and nap, but he hasn't been able to sleep with you preaching. And some of the people don't like you. You don't flatter them enough. You do not mix well, Amos. Neither are you as dignified as you should be. We have noticed that you pound the pulpit. That is very crude in Bethel. We do not like your emotional outbursts. We never get excited about religion here. And by the way, Amos, did you ever study homiletics? Your messages lack organization. You need a course in public speaking, which will train you to speak with a deep voice in a very dignified manner so that you can say nothing as if it were something. Amos, you are no longer welcome at Bethel."

Now the answer of Amos reveals the heart of this prophet.

> **Then Amos answered, and said to Amaziah: "I was no prophet, nor was I a son of a prophet, but I was a sheepbreeder and a tender of sycamore fruit. Then the Lord took me as I followed the flock, and the Lord said to me, 'Go, prophesy to My people Israel.'"**
> (Amos 7:14–15)

Friend, that is not the answer of a fanatic, is it? It is a soft answer. You may think he is crude by the way he dresses, but his answer reveals refinement. Looking back over twenty-five hundred years, he stands in better light than does Amaziah. It is the gracious answer of a gentleman.

There is only one criticism I can make of Amos, and

I trust I will be forgiven for making this one. He is naive; he is artless; he is frank; he is just a babe-in-the-woods in Bethel. Down yonder in the desert wilderness of Tekoa, he knew his way around. He could travel through the darkness of that desert guided by the stars. Read his prophecy and you will find that he knew those stars well. He knew about the roar of a lion, then the scream of a helpless animal that had fallen into its clutches. He refers to this in his prophecy. He knew the telltale movement in the brush and the hiss of a venomous serpent. He was at home in the jungle filled with wild animals, but in the asphalt jungle of Bethel he was helpless.

If someone will just lead Amos around and say, "Amos, there is the roar of a lion!"

"Roar of a lion? I don't hear the roar of a lion, and I *know* lions."

"Yes, but up here in Bethel that lion is Mr. Gotrocks. He didn't like that message you gave because the shoe fit him, and he is roaring from the pinch. He's a lion. He has influence. He will eat you up!"

"You don't mean to tell me that a Christian brother . . . why, I'm giving God's message . . . he wouldn't eat me up, would he?"

"Be careful, Amos; don't step there. You almost stepped on a serpent!"

"Serpent? I don't see a serpent. All I see is Mrs. Joe Doaks. You don't mean to tell me . . ."

"Yes, she is a serpent in this asphalt jungle. The poison of asps is under her lips, and with her tongue she uses deceit. She has bitten and poisoned many people. Be careful, Amos!"

Amos is naive. He doesn't know his way around in Bethel. But listen to his credentials.

Then the LORD took me as I followed the flock, and the LORD said to me, "Go, prophesy to My people Israel."
(Amos 7:15)

Amos is saying, "I never claimed to be a preacher. I was not taught in the schools of the prophets. As for homiletics—what is it? I have never heard of it. I only know that when I was down in that wilderness of Tekoa, walking with God, one day He called me and gave me a message. His message was like a burning fire in my bones, and He said, 'Go to Bethel and deliver it.' That is what I am doing here. You preachers who have come to me, you are not angry, are you? You are not against God's Word, are you?"

Oh, Amos, how can you be so simple? They do not want the Word of God in Bethel.

My friend, as we read the prophecy of Amos, we see that it is against sin. Amos preached against sin. Years ago I asked Homer Rodeheaver when I was with him at Winona Lake Bible Conference on one occasion, "You were with Billy Sunday for a long time. What was the secret of that man's ministry?" We were sitting together at a table. He laid down his knife and fork with which he was carving, reached over, and tapped me on the arm. In his very winsome manner, he said, "Billy Sunday preached against sin. The trouble today is that preachers do not preach against sin." I have not forgotten that. This also was the secret of the ministry of Amos. He preached against sin. He was not a mealy-mouthed preacher. He did not give out messages of saccharine sweetness, artificial light, and ersatz bread. He gave the real article.

Yet to him God was a God of love. But He was not soft and sentimental and shallow. He was a God who punished sin. Amos did not deal with vague generalities. Some time ago I heard this said of a preacher, "He preaches that you must repent, as it were; believe, in a measure; or be lost, to some extent." Oh, how indefinite some preaching can be! But this man Amos went right to the point.

There were three areas about which he spoke. Out of these three situations in his land, he brought a message. It was a day of prosperity in Israel. During the reign of Jeroboam II, great prosperity had come and the people were living in luxury. In the sixth chapter of Amos' prophecy he says:

> **Woe to you who are at ease in Zion. . . . who lie on beds of ivory, stretch out on your couches, eat lambs from the flock and calves from the midst of the stall.**
> (Amos 6:1, 4)

As they reclined upon their foam rubber couches, they enjoyed filet mignon one night, and the next night they feasted on lamb chops. Amos continues:

> **Who sing idly to the sound of stringed instruments, and invent for yourselves musical instruments . . .**
> (Amos 6:5)

Their music, like that of America, was taking them farther and farther away from God. Then Amos mentions the third thing:

Who drink wine from bowls . . .
(Amos 6:6)

They were not satisfied with a little glass of wine—they drank it from *bowls*. It was a day of drunkenness.

The message of Amos is a modern message. These are the things that are destroying America today. Prosperity has brought luxury and greed, our music gives us away, and we are becoming a nation of drunkards. Israel's sins are America's sins.

And simply because they were being religious on the surface did not guarantee that God would not judge their sin. Because of their rejection of His law, their deceit and robbery and violence and oppression of the poor, God said,

I hate, I despise your feast days. . . . Though you offer Me burnt offerings and your grain offerings, I will not accept them. . . . Take away from Me the noise of your songs. . . . But let justice run down like water, and righteousness like a mighty stream.
(Amos 5:21–24)

It was a day of false peace. In the north was hanging Assyria like the sword of Damocles, ready to fall; and in the next half century, Assyria would indeed destroy this little kingdom. Isreal was trying to ignore it, and they kept talking about peace; but Amos said,

> **Behold, the eyes of the Lord GOD are on the sinful kingdom, and I will destroy it from the face of the earth; . . .**
> (Amos 9:8)

His message was not a popular message. He warned that God intends to punish sin.

However, this man Amos had a long-range view, and I conclude with this verse:

> **On that day I will raise up the tabernacle of David, which has fallen down, and repair its damages; I will raise up its ruins, and rebuild it as in the days of old.**
> (Amos 9:11)

Amos, looking down into the future, saw that God, by mercy and by grace, was going to yet redeem His people. He saw something that James saw at that great council at Jerusalem centuries later. When James cited an Old Testament prophecy about what was taking place, he did not go to Isaiah, he did not go to David, neither did he go to Moses. He went to the prophecy of Amos where God had said,

> **After this I will return and will rebuild the tabernacle of David, which has fallen down . . . .**
> (Acts 15:16)

But beyond that which Amos saw, James realized that now out of the Gentiles God is calling a people to His name. And just as He dealt with Israel in mercy, He will deal with all people in mercy if they will have it.

God can be merciful because our Lord Jesus Christ, when He came to Zion, was not at ease. He said, "My Father has been working until now, and I have been working" (John 5:17). It was at Zion that He wept over the city of Jerusalem. It was there that He was beaten. It was there that He was led out of the city. It was there that He was crucified. Christ was not at ease in Zion so that through His death God might be merciful and bring rest to you. He was not at ease because God is not willing that any should perish; but they *will* perish if they will not have His mercy. This is the simple message of Amos.

God has not changed. He is the same yesterday, today, and forever. He will punish sin.

But He says,

Come now, and let us reason together, . . . though your sins are like scarlet, they shall be as white as snow; though they are red like crimson, they shall be as wool.
(Isaiah 1:18)

My friend, don't laugh at the country preacher. He has a message from God. Many of the sophisticates and intellectuals in Amos' day were wrong. They can be wrong in our day as well. God still says, "Come now, and let us reason together. . . ." But don't be deceived. God is not soft. God is not sentimental. God will punish sin—but He will forgive the sinner who turns to Him.

6

JONAH: DEAD OR ALIVE?

Part 1

PASSAGE TO TARSHISH

Now the word of the LORD came to Jonah the son of Amittai, saying, "Arise, go to Nineveh, that great city, and cry out against it; for their wickedness has come up before Me." But Jonah arose to flee to Tarshish from the presence of the LORD. He went down to Joppa, and found a ship going to Tarshish; so he paid the fare, and went down into it, to go with them to Tarshish from the presence of the LORD. But the LORD sent out a great wind on the sea, and there was a mighty tempest on the sea, so that the ship was about to be broken up. Then the mariners were afraid; and every man cried out to his god, and threw the cargo that was in the ship

into the sea, to lighten the load. But Jonah had gone down into the lowest parts of the ship, had lain down, and was fast asleep.
(Jonah 1:1–5)

The little Book of Jonah is one to which I have given a great deal of attention. When I was in seminary, the higher critics leveled their guns against the Book of Jonah more than against any other book in the Bible. Of course, the explanation that has been offered and is still offered today by some is that Jonah never existed, that he was only a myth. They classify his story in the realm of Aesop's fables and fairy tales. Although the critic has been hard put to come up with any reasonable explanation of Jonah, there have been some very interesting and humorous attempts. Some critics have said, without a scrap of evidence to support it, that Jonah was the son of the widow of Zarephath. There's no reason in the world for saying that other than her son was raised from the dead.

And then the theory is put forth that Jonah actually did live and that he did take a trip by ship but had a dream while he was sleeping, and the events recorded in the Book of Jonah are an account of the dream. There's no evidence, of course, to support this theory either.

Then there are those who believe that the Book of Jonah corresponds to the Phoenician myth of Hercules and the sea monster. Again, there's no evidence at all for that claim.

Others suggest that Jonah really lived, that he took

a trip by ship, that there was a storm, and that the ship was wrecked. Then, they say, he was picked up by another ship that had as its figurehead a fish on its bow, and so Jonah thought he was picked up by a fish. Someone really had an imagination to come up with that one, and certainly you have to be gullible to accept it!

There are others who make the wild claim that Jonah went through all the experiences described in the Book of Jonah until he was wrecked, and then he took refuge in a dead fish floating around. That is their explanation of how he got to land! The only thing is, they have it in reverse. We believe it was not the fish that was dead; it was Jonah who was dead inside the fish. We'll see that as we go along.

In the Old Testament I consider each one of the twelve so-called minor prophets as a little nuclear bomb. They are not *minor* prophets at all; they all batted in the major league. Each one of them has a terrific message. The little Book of Jonah has several messages, as we're going to see.

While the Book of Jonah is not a prophetic book, the writer Jonah was a prophet, and he gave a prophecy. The very interesting thing is that the prophecy he gave *did not* come true. Yet I have never heard a critic find fault with him for giving a prophecy that didn't come true. Jonah said, "Yet forty days, and Nineveh shall be overthrown!" (Jonah 3:4). But it was not destroyed in forty days. It was a hundred years later that the city of Nineveh was destroyed. However, may I say that Jonah was speaking by the Spirit of God when he said what he did; therefore, it was fulfilled according to the Word of God. That will become clear near the end of the story, as we shall see.

Grasping the Message

I was about sixteen years old when I was saved, but I had not been brought up in a Christian home and was never taught anything concerning the Word of God. Probably no one ever went to seminary as ignorant of the Bible as I was, but I wanted to get a hold on the Bible and try to understand it. I found out that it met my purposes if I could outline the books of the Bible.

I have to admit that the most difficult portions of the Bible for me to outline were these little minor prophets. Even the last time through, when I tried to reoutline the Book of Hosea, I took it up six different times and put it down without being satisfied at all. It seemed as though the message that was there eluded me each time. Also I had a great deal of difficulty in trying to outline the Book of Jonah.

Then one night many years ago, I was waiting for a train in Nashville, Tennessee, and I did what you probably do. Trying to kill time, I walked around and looked at everything. When I came to the timetable, all of a sudden it occurred to me that the Book of Jonah should be divided according to a timetable such as you find in a union station or in an airport. There are three things that are always essential for a timetable: the destination of the train or the plane, the time it leaves, and the time it arrives. Those are the three things that you always look for.

So, I've divided the four chapters of the little Book of Jonah like that. In chapter 1 the destination of Jonah is Nineveh. He leaves his hometown of Gath Hepher in the Northern Kingdom of Israel, and he arrives in the fish. And then in chapter 2 his destination is still Nineveh. He leaves the fish and arrives on the dry land. In chapter 3 the destination is still Nineveh. He leaves the dry land and arrives in Nineveh. Chapter 4 gives his destination as outside the city of Nineveh. He leaves Nineveh, and he arrives in the heart of God. May I say, that's a marvelous place for a backsliding prophet, a backsliding preacher, or a backsliding Christian to arrive—in the heart of God. That is the message, I believe, of the little Book of Jonah.

Now let me give just a word concerning the existence of this man. The text begins, "Now the word of the LORD came to Jonah the son of Amittai. . . ." He is identified for us here. Actually, we know more about Jonah than we do about most of the minor prophets. For instance, the prophecy of Obadiah that precedes Jonah tells us nothing about his person. Yet as far as I know there is not a critic who questions his existence. Isn't it strange that they question the existence of Jonah but not Obadiah, when there's not a historical record of Obadiah at all?

Well, we do know something about this man Jonah. There is an historical record in 2 Kings in connection with Jeroboam the son of Joash who was the king at that time. It says:

He [Jeroboam] restored the territory of Israel from the entrance of Hamath to the Sea of the Arabah, according to the word of the LORD God of Israel, which He had

spoken through his servant Jonah the son of Amittai, the prophet who was from Gath Hepher.
(2 Kings 14:25)

This is a clear historical reference to Jonah. First of all, his name is *Jonah*; second, he's the son of Amittai; and third, Amittai was a prophet. These three points of identification prove that this is the same man as in the book which bears his name. He's an historical character.

Many years ago, when I was much younger, I used to play handball with a very liberal preacher in Nashville, Tennessee. One day after we had finished playing and were sitting in the locker room resting, he said to me, "I saw in the paper where you were preaching on Jonah."

"Yes."

"You don't really believe he existed!"

"Yes."

"What proof do you have?"

So I gave him this reference, 2 Kings 14:25. Frankly, that stumped him because he'd never had that called to his attention before. Well, he came back the next time we played and said, "I think that's a different Jonah."

I told him, "Well, it's possible there could have been two Jonahs. But the interesting thing is Jonah was an unusual name; it's not *Jones* but *Jonah*. The telephone book may be full of Joneses but not Jonahs."

But this preacher still insisted that it was a different Jonah; so I said, "Well, you're just like Mark Twain, relative to the argument about Shakespeare." As you may know, the same argument goes on about

Shakespeare. Many fine students of literature do not believe Shakespeare wrote Shakespeare. They think Francis Bacon or somebody else wrote it. And Mark Twain's wry comment was, "Shakespeare did not write Shakespeare. It was written by another man by the same name." And that's what we have here. We have "Jonah the son of Amittai," and if you think this is another Jonah, then it's another Jonah by the same name. Therefore, I believe that we have an historical character here in the Book of Jonah.

Now if that were not enough, we also have an authority. As far as I'm concerned, when the Lord Jesus Christ says it, it's final for me, and I have no other place to appeal. He made two very definite references to Jonah, which we'll be looking at later, but in Luke 11:30 our Lord says,

For as Jonah became a sign to the Ninevites, so also the Son of Man will be to this generation.

This Jonah was a sign. Now there could not have been another man who lived as a sign. Our Lord treated him as an historical character, and I believe He was in a better position to know than any man in any seminary or university today. He is the authority, and this record in the Book of Jonah actually took place.

Purpose of the Book

Let's look at the record that's given to us here. We are told,

Now the word of the LORD came to Jonah the son of Amittai, saying, "Arise, go to Nineveh, that great city, and cry out against it; for their wickedness has come up before Me."
(Jonah 1:1–2)

God wanted to *save* Nineveh!

At the tower of Babel, God bade the world as a whole good-bye in order to concentrate on one family. In substance He said, "I'll have to leave you for a time, because I have to prepare a redemption for you." And that redemption came through the line of Abraham. I wonder if you have ever noticed how the New Testament opens: "The book of the genealogy of Jesus Christ, the Son of David, the Son of Abraham" (Matthew 1:1). That genealogy is all-important.

God has prepared a redemption for man. The little Book of Jonah, in my judgment, is God saying to the world in the interval from the tower of Babel to the coming of Christ, "I haven't forgotten you. I'll save you if you will turn to Me." The Book of Jonah speaks of the most wicked, brutal people who have ever lived on this earth—the Assyrians. Even secular history says that about them. Yet God saved them! And if God would save them, He would save anyone who would turn to Him. This entire city turned to God, and God saved them!

Problems With Jonah

God says to this man Jonah, "Arise, go to Nineveh, that great city, and cry out against it; for their wickedness has come up before Me." This is where the problem begins. My problem is not with the fish. I think it's nonsense to make that an issue today. The fish is only one of the props; it's incidental. We do well to keep separate the essentials and the incidentals. The essentials are Jonah and Jehovah. The fish is only a by-product.

But I'm having trouble now with Jonah:

But Jonah arose to flee to Tarshish from the presence of the LORD. He went down to Joppa, and found a ship going to Tarshish; so he paid the fare, and went down into it, to go with them to Tarshish from the presence of the LORD.
(Jonah 1:3)

And may I say, this upsets our theology. Will you notice, here is a prophet of God! God calls him to go to Nineveh. Nineveh is in the northeast—east by north. And this man goes in the opposite direction. He goes down to Joppa; he buys a ticket for Tarshish, which was in Spain, the jumping-off place of the world in that day. It was believed that you couldn't go any farther west than Tarshish, and if you sailed out through the Pillars of Hercules you would sail off the earth and perish. So Jonah bought a ticket for a place as far away as he could go.

Now the thing that disturbs me is this: Here is a prophet of God who has been called to go in one direction, so why does he go in another direction? Why in the world didn't the man do what God called him to do?

Well, there are several explanations I can offer, and you can accept one of them or all of them. First of all let me say that this man Jonah hated Ninevites. I mean, he *hated* them with a passion. He did not want them saved, and he had a reason for this. We do know that in the days of Jonah the Northern Kingdom of Israel was subject to attack by Assyria. Certain detachments of the army were making forays down into the Northern Kingdom. They would capture an entire town and kill many of the inhabitants. And while I do not know this, I suspect that Jonah was living in his hometown of Gath Hepher in the Northern Kingdom when the Assyrians came. He may have seen his own mother and father slain before his eyes and maybe brothers and sisters taken away captive. Perhaps as a little fellow he witnessed all of that from some shelter where he was hiding. I do know this, he *hated* Ninevites. He did not want them saved, and so he went in the opposite direction, away from Nineveh. That's one reason.

Then the second reason is, God never asked any Old Testament prophet to go as a witness to the world. Have you ever noticed that? The fact of the matter is, one of the great distinctions between Israel in the Old Testament and the church in the New Testament is the direction they are to go. God never said to the prophets of Israel, "Go into all the world and preach the gospel to every creature." Rather, He said, "I want you to talk to My people." He said, "I want you to speak to My people right here." Their invitation was "Come, let us go up to the house of the LORD." And, my friend, the world came. The queen of Sheba came from the ends of the earth. We like to say today that Israel failed and the church has succeeded. I think it would be more accurate to turn it around.

In the days of Solomon, the kings of the earth came to hear the wisdom of Solomon, and the Scripture says they came to see "the ascent" or the entryway that he had. What was that? It was that entry to the burnt altar where a sacrifice that pointed to Jesus Christ was offered for sin. I say to you, Israel witnessed to the world by having the world come to them.

And Jonah could have said, "Look here, Lord, You never told Elijah to go up to Nineveh, and he was a big, brave man. Why do You ask me to do something you've never asked any other prophet to do?" And I think Jonah would have had justification for that.

There's a third reason, and this one will disturb you. Do you want to know why? Look down in your own heart today. We have a commission to take the glorious news of Jesus Christ to the ends of the earth. Why are we going in the opposite direction? Let's don't talk about Jonah disobeying God when, as a whole, we have miserably failed in taking the gospel out to the lost world. Examine your own heart right now, and you'll understand the human side of Jonah. We are not busy carrying out our commission either. I'm not going to criticize Jonah. I just have some problems with him, that's all.

Here is a man to whom God says, "I want you to go to Nineveh." That's to the east. Jonah says, "I'm going to Tarshish; I'm going west." And that's where he headed.

And will you notice something else that is here. He

found a ship going to Tarshish, so he paid the fare and went down into it "to go with them to Tarshish from the presence of the LORD." Now when he talked to the sailors, one of the things he probably said was that he was sure it was God's will for him to go to Tarshish now because the door opened. Oh, have I heard that! "I know the Lord is leading me because everything has been so easy!" Is that the way God leads? I don't think so. I hear that today; then later I hear of the tragedy at the end of the road, and I wonder whether God was really leading or not.

My friend, may I say to you that when God leads He does not always lead through pathways strewn with flowers. He doesn't always lead down a gentle slope with the stones removed from your path. Read the story of Abraham. He did well in Ur of the Chaldees until God called him, and then he started having trouble. But just because someone is having trouble doesn't mean he is out of God's will. And just because everything is going easy in your life doesn't mean, my friend, you're in God's will. So often I hear today: "We know God is leading us because we prayed about this, and the door just opened, and everything else worked out beautifully for us." It did? Well hallelujah for you, brother. But I didn't find it easy. And I don't find it easy today. I'm disturbed when I hear other Christians tell me how easy they're having it. That's *not* a sign God is leading you.

Good old Jonah! Can you imagine him going down to Joppa to the shipping company office and getting in the line of people buying their tickets? Right ahead of him is a man saying, "Do you have a ticket for Tarshish?" The agent shakes his head. "Sorry, all my reservations have

been taken." Well, Jonah is just about ready to turn away when the phone rings and the agent turns to answer it. And Jonah hears him say, "You mean that you can't go, Mr. Smith? Well that's too bad." When he turns around again to the window Jonah says, "Well, I don't know whether to ask it or not, but do you have a ticket for Tarshish?" And the agent says, "Are you lucky! You are *so* lucky! A man just cancelled, and I'm going to let you have his reservation. I can give you a first-class cabin." Jonah pays the fare, and he goes down to the ship singing, "Praise the Lord!" I say to you, I have trouble with Jonah because, my friend, that isn't the way God seems to do it. This man's going to be in a lot of trouble before this trip is over!

You may remember the apostle Paul's final voyage to Rome and his encounter with a storm (Acts 27). He counseled the captain of that ship not to go on. But when "the south wind blew softly," the captain ignored Paul's advice. You be careful when the south wind is blowing softly, Christian. May I say to you, that's right before the storm. My dad used to say in west Texas when we had to go to the storm cellar at night, "It's time to go!" And as kids we'd say, "But, Dad, it's quiet now." He would insist, "This is the time to go. It's the quiet before the storm hits."

Jonah found everything so nice and easy. And in this affluent society today I'm hearing so many people say, "The Lord is leading us." Is He? How do you know? "Well, everything is so easy!" May I say again, the south wind blows softly. But you should have seen the storm that the apostle Paul got in! The ship was

wrecked. And if Paul had not been there everyone on board would have lost his life. They did lose the cargo.

However, in Jonah's case notice who was responsible for the storm.

But the LORD sent out a great wind on the sea, and there was a mighty tempest on the sea, so that the ship was about to be broken up.
(Jonah 1:4)

This storm was supernatural; and these sailors sensed that, by the way.

It was also a supernatural storm that the devil used to try to destroy our Lord. You remember that Jesus was asleep in the boat, and the disciples on board were fishermen who knew the Sea of Galilee. They could have handled any boat in any storm they'd ever seen on that body of water, but this one they couldn't handle. Finally, in desperation they went and waked Him, "Teacher, do You not care that we are perishing?" (Mark 4:38). It was a supernatural storm.

And this is a supernatural storm that Jonah is in, as we shall see.

Then the mariners were afraid; and every man cried out to his god, and threw the cargo that was in the ship into the sea, to lighten the load. But Jonah had gone down into the lowest parts of the ship, had lain down, and was fast asleep.
(Jonah 1:5)

I find this troubling too. I have been told by the saints, "If you are a child of God, and you get out of the will of

God, you won't be able to sleep at night; your conscience will bother you." Oh? Jonah, a backsliding prophet, called to go to Nineveh, is on the way to Tarshish, out of the will of God, and he's fast asleep! And the interesting thing is, he's the only man on board who is asleep! Everybody else is scared to death. My, how often I have heard it said, "If you get out of the will of God, Christian friend, your conscience will bother you."

May I say this to you, and I want to say it very carefully, there are Christians who have been out of the will of God for years, and they never miss a night's sleep. Their conscience doesn't bother them. They have been out of His will for so long that they can even let obvious sins come in their lives, and it doesn't disturb them. They go on keeping up a front. We have to keep up a front before the other saints, you know! God have mercy on us today that we can have a conscience so seared that we can tolerate this in our lives. We can be spiritually cold and indifferent, and it doesn't bother us.

Poor old Jonah, he's asleep! Everybody else is wide awake and frantic, and he is sleeping!

Jonah: Dead or Alive?
Part 2

GOING THE WRONG WAY ON A ONE-WAY STREET

Using Jonah as an example, may I say to you, we ought to be very sure when we get on board ship that we are in God's will. I talked to a couple here several years ago who were going to the mission field. I questioned them, "Are you sure this is what God wants you to do?" Oh yes, they had God's leading! And what they told me was His leading is not leading at all; but they thought it was. I'm sorry to say, they came back inside of a year. They were casualties. They will never go to the mission field again, I'm confident. My friend, before you buy your ticket, be sure that you're in the will of God. We need to do a great deal of testing today concerning that.

Now there is a storm breaking over this boat because there is a backsliding prophet aboard.

So the captain came to him, and said to him, "What do you mean, sleeper? Arise, call on your God; perhaps your God will consider us, so that we may not perish." (Jonah 1:6)

This is embarrassing for Jonah. Imagine having the pagan captain of that ship come down and rebuke him because he is the one asleep—and he should have been leading the prayer meeting! May I say to you, Jonah is far from God. He's really out of fellowship with God, and yet he could sleep.

A lot of Christians are asleep as well. It doesn't bother them that they're out of fellowship with Him. I'm sure that a great many people on the outside observing Christians today would say under their breath, "If I believed as you believe, I wouldn't live like you are living." Well, this captain doesn't mind rebuking Jonah.

> **And they said to one another, "Come, let us cast lots, that we may know for whose cause this trouble has come upon us."**
> (Jonah 1:7)

These sailors are accustomed to the Mediterranean, and they detect that this is no *natural* storm.

> **. . . So they cast lots, and the lot fell on Jonah. Then they said to him, "Please tell us! For whose cause is this trouble upon us? What is your occupation? And where do you come from? What is your country? And of what people are you?"**
> (Jonah 1:7–8)

They cast lots to find out why or who on board is responsible. The critic has said, "That's superstition!" And if you want to know my view, superstition is exactly what it was. Somebody says, "You mean to tell me that God is going to use that?" Yes, God is going to use superstition to accomplish His purpose. We have several examples of this in the Word of God. In the days of Moses, when God carried on a battle with Pharaoh, He dealt with him in terms he could understand. Every one of the plagues was leveled at a particular idol in the land of Egypt. God communicated down on their level.

And when God wanted to speak to Nebuchadnezzar, the king of Babylon who worshiped idols, how did He speak to him? Through an idol, that multimetallic image he saw in his dream. God came down to his level. And God used that method also with His own people. I've always wanted to know what the urim and the thummim were in the high priest's garments. I'm confident that they were used in determining the will of God. Now somebody again is going to say, "You don't mean to tell me that God's people used something mechanical?" Yes. Let me ask you, child of God, how do you determine the will of God? I know some folk who come at it like this: They open the Bible at random with their eyes closed, then read the first verse they see. And whatever it is, that's going to be God's will for them. Now don't laugh, because many Christians have used that method. In fact, I have used it.

Many years ago when I was considering a call to a certain church, I put my Bible under my arm one night and told my wife, "I'm going over to the study, and I'm not going to leave it until I know what God's will is for me." So I went over there, and I got down on my knees and said, "Lord, I'm staying here until You show me." And I should probably still be there because I don't think He did show me. But I opened the Bible and turned to a verse which was, "Woe to the worthless [or idle] shepherd who leaves the flock! . . ." (Zechariah 11:17). I took that as meaning I wasn't to go to the church that had called me, and I'm sure I made a mistake by using that method.

Now I'll grant that this type of thing is superstition, but I have discovered that God sometimes uses these methods. I'm of the opinion today that God is wanting to communicate with the human family more than He has ever wanted to before. I'm confident of that. And I think God uses many methods today to direct us. Let me give you one more illustration of how He can use superstition.

When I was pastor in Nashville, Tennessee, we had in the Sunday school one of the most precious little girls I've ever seen. Every now and then one of those comes along, a Miss Personality, an attractive child whom everybody notices. And she had the meanest father that I've ever met. He was a godless man. The child came to Sunday school, and twice a year she'd bring him to church—on Christmas and on Easter. At the first Christmas she told me that he was going to come, and I alerted everybody to be sure and shake hands with him and make him feel at home. And they did. So his criticism was, "They make over you too much in that church. I don't like it." His little daughter had told me this; so at Eastertime I said to the folk, "This time rather ignore him, because he doesn't like to be made over." And after the service he made the statement, "They're certainly a cold crowd in that church. They're not friendly at all." You can't win with a fellow like that! It was my first pastorate, and I went by his home one day to talk to him about the Lord. That was a great mistake. He ordered me out of his house. He said, "I do not want to talk to you about that. My religion is my business, and I don't intend to talk to you at all." And so I just decided that this man was beyond being reached.

But then it happened. He ran a dry cleaning place, and he had a cashier working for him who told him one morning, "I went to a fortune teller last night."

"You did? What did she say?"

"Well, I'll tell you what she said. She told me that I was going to die suddenly, be killed accidentally, and that the man I work for would die shortly after that."

A few days later that woman stepped off a streetcar, and an automobile that didn't stop for the unloading of passengers hit her and killed her. You know what that unsaved fellow began to think—that he was next! He believed that his time was short, and he became desperate. One night in the manse where I lived I heard the door rattle so loud I thought somebody was knocking it down. When I opened the door I had never seen such a wild-eyed man as he was. He came in, and he said, "I want to talk with you."

"What do you want to talk about?"

"I want to talk about getting saved. You wanted to talk to me about it; now I want to listen."

"Well, what brought you to this?" And he told me the story about his cashier. He said, "I guess I'm next, and I want to get right with God." Then he said, "You were talking about dispensations when my daughter brought me to the church one night, and frankly I was a little interested in that. Would you explain it to me again, because that sort of began to open the Bible to me." So I got a piece of brown wrapping paper and a pencil, and we both got down on our knees on the floor while I drew a chart of the dispensations like I always use. We went from the dispensation of creation to the dispensation of innocence, the dispensation of conscience, then promise, then the Law, and then we came to grace. And that's when I began to talk to him about the fact that God, in this age of grace, was asking of man nothing but faith, that we need only to trust Christ as Savior. When I looked up from the chart and into the face of this man, I saw by his expression that he was ready to be saved. So I said to him, "Wouldn't you right now like to accept Christ as your Savior?" He said, "I sure would." We didn't even have to get down on our knees because we were already on our knees; and that man, right there and then, received Jesus Christ as his Savior.

He became, may I say, a different man. I knew he was converted because he began to come to all the services, and he laughed at my jokes after that! My friend, God used superstition. He used a fortune teller who, to my judgment, was as big a fake as they come. Her prediction just happened to work out for the cashier. But it was the means of bringing to Christ that man, the father of a precious child in our Sunday school. I'm confident nothing else would ever have brought him to the Lord. You say to me, "This was superstition." Sure it was, and God will get down to your level if it means reaching you, my friend.

Now back in the days of Jonah, God used the superstition of casting lots to reach a bunch of pagan sailors. When the lot fell on Jonah, they began pelting him with questions.

Then they said to him, "Please tell us! For whose cause is this trouble upon us? What is your occupation? And where do you come from? What is your country? And of what people are you?"
(Jonah 1:8)

Jonah was a talkative fellow. It seems that he had talked a lot when he first came aboard, but he hadn't told them the thing he should have told them. We don't hear him telling them that God could save them. Apparently he was not a witness for God. They never would have asked him what nationality he was if he had said he was a Hebrew, since a Hebrew was a Hebrew because of his religion as much as his nationality. And if Jonah had just said to them, "I'm a Hebrew," it would have opened the door for him to witness; but he hadn't said that. Instead he talked about other things. It's amazing when you are out of fellowship with God that you don't want to talk about Him—any more than the unsaved man wants to talk about Him, by the way. And you're not a very good witness at that time.

Now will you listen:

So he said to them, "I am a Hebrew. . . ."

and that gave it all away,

" . . . and I fear the LORD, the God of heaven, who made the sea and the dry land."
(Jonah 1:9)

These men were idolaters. They worshiped the sun, moon, and stars. Now Jonah tells them that he does not worship these things, but he worships the Creator of these things, the Maker.

Then the men were exceedingly afraid, and said to him, "Why have you done

this?" For the men knew that he fled from the presence of the LORD, because he had told them.
(Jonah 1:10)

When you, as a child of God, are out of the will of God, you'll rationalize your actions. And if you rationalize your actions, you're going to confide in somebody. Have you ever done that? You're not sure about what you're doing, so you go and talk it over with somebody—maybe a friend or your pastor. I'm confident that a great many folk who have come to me for counseling did not want my advice. They only wanted me to agree with what they had already decided to do. You see, they were rationalizing, and they wanted to get me over on their side.

I have a notion that when the ship got underway Jonah stepped up to the pilot and said, "How do you like your job?" The pilot said, "Fine. Where are you going?"

"Well, I'm going all the way with you. I'm going to Tarshish."

"Ever been there?"

"No, never been there."

"Well, you're going to find out that's a jumping-off place. It is way out there."

"I know, but I'll let you in on something. I've really been called to go up to Nineveh, but the way I look at it . . ."

When anybody starts talking to you like that, you know he is rationalizing. "The way I look at it is that I should not go to Nineveh. To begin with, I don't care for Ninevites at all. Do you know anything about those people?"

"Yes, this ship was attacked by the Ninevites."

"What?"

"Yes, we got away from them, but they got another ship, and they killed every sailor."

"Well then, you understand my feelings of not wanting to go to Nineveh."

The pilot patted him on the back. "I think you're doing the right thing," and Jonah went away feeling good, so good he could fall fast asleep.

Man Overboard

But now in the midst of the storm, Jonah is on deck and has been singled out as the reason for the ship's terrible predicament.

> **Then they said to him, "What shall we do to you that the sea may be calm for us?"—for the sea was growing more tempestuous.**
> (Jonah 1:11)

You see, these men are moving cautiously. Actually, these pagans show up much better than Jonah does here at the beginning.

> **And he said to them, "Pick me up and throw me into the sea; then the sea will become calm for you. For I know that this great tempest is because of me."**
> (Jonah 1:12)

Jonah knew now that God was speaking to him.

"Nevertheless the men rowed hard to return to land. . . ." I'm sure some would say these pagan sailors were uncivilized, but they act very civilized to me. They did not want to throw Jonah overboard. Do you notice, he said to them, "Throw me into the sea." In their hearts they were saying, "Oh, no; not that! We'll make another effort to try to get this boat into port somewhere."

> **Nevertheless the men rowed hard to return to land, but they could not, for the sea continued to grow more tempestuous against them. Therefore they cried out to the LORD and said, . . .**
> (Jonah 1:13–14)

Do you notice what's happening? They're crying out now to the Lord! Something did happen, didn't it? These pagan sailors are not bowing down to an idol to ask for mercy, nor are they entreating the sun, moon, and stars; but they're speaking now to the Creator.

> **. . . "We pray, O LORD, please do not let us perish for this man's life, and do not charge us with innocent blood; for You, O LORD, have done as it pleased You."**
> (Jonah 1:14)

In other words, they are calling upon God to forgive them for what they are going to do because they have no alternative.

> **So they picked up Jonah and threw him into the sea, and the sea ceased from its raging.**
> (Jonah 1:15)

You can be sure these men were startled at the sudden calm! This was a positive confirmation that the storm was supernatural.

> **Then the men feared the LORD exceedingly, and offered a sacrifice to the LORD and took vows.**
> (Jonah 1:16)

Did they fear their gods? No. They feared the One who is the Creator of the sea and of the land.

I believe these men came to a knowledge of the living and true God. They did two things: They made "a sacrifice to the LORD." I believe that sacrifice, which was obviously a burnt sacrifice, pointed to the Lord Jesus Christ. And I believe that in the best way they could, with the little knowledge they had, they looked in faith to God.

And then it says they "took vows." A vow in the Old Testament was very important. I had this impressed on my mind when studying the Book of Leviticus. And the writer of the Proverbs says that when you make a vow to God you be sure that you pay it, because if you don't, He will hold you to it. God doesn't like anyone making an idle vow to Him, and that's my reason today for believing that we ought to be very careful of what we promise God. Oh, how many people under the emotion of the moment make a promise to God that they never keep. I believe God holds us to our vows.

These sailors made vows, which means in Old Testament language that they not only came to the true God at this time with a sacrifice, but they also promised to serve Him. And I think we have a right to believe that these men, through this tremendous experience, turned to the living and true God. So something good was accomplished by the storm, by Jonah's being on board the ship, and by his being cast overboard. But the mariners disappear over the horizon, and we do not know what actually happened to them.

But I do know what happened to Jonah.

Now the LORD had prepared a great fish to swallow Jonah. And Jonah was in the belly of the fish three days and three nights.
(Jonah 1:17)

Here is the crux of this story. It has been assumed that Jonah spent three days and three nights inside the fish like you would spend a weekend in a comfortable motel—that somehow or other he spent three days alive inside the fish.

Years ago I took the position, which I still hold today, that Jonah was not alive inside the fish but that he died and God raised him from the dead. I have been verbally attacked for this position. In fact, a theological professor in this area said that because Jonah was a backsliding prophet he could not have been a type of Christ. And yet this same professor taught that King David is a type of Christ! I think Jonah makes a better type of Christ than David, if you're going to measure him by the sin in his life. Neither of them is a type of Christ when it comes to their sin or their backsliding. Jonah is a type in only one area, and that is in his death and resurrection. And that's the way the Lord Jesus put it when He was asked for a sign. He said,

> **An evil and adulterous generation seeks after a sign, and no sign will be given to it except the sign of the prophet Jonah. For as Jonah was three days and three nights in the belly of the great fish, so will the Son of Man be three days and three nights in the heart of the earth.**
> (Matthew 12:39–40)

Now, my friend, was the Lord Jesus alive or dead? "Well," you say, "He was dead for three days." Yes. Was Jonah alive or dead? He had to be dead in order to bear out what our Lord is saying. I do not think that the Scripture passage makes it clear that this man was alive for the three days.

And then may I add this: If I'm wrong, and Jonah was alive—and if in heaven someday Jonah comes up to me and says, "Boy, did you misrepresent me!"—then I want to say to him, "I'm very sorry, Jonah. But you should have made it lots more clear for this poor preacher."

If Jonah had stayed alive inside the fish, that would not have been a miracle. You say, "Not a miracle?" No. Did you know that other men have been swallowed by fish and have lived to tell the story? It's nonsense for anyone to argue that it's impossible for a fish to swallow a man whole. I have read of seven or eight instances. In fact, there are several accounts on record of men being swallowed by large fish and living to tell

the tale. Grace W. Kellogg, in her excellent little book-
let on the subject, *The Bible Today*, has compiled a list
of the records—which have been authenticated—of the
experiences of living creatures in fish who later were
rescued alive. We are quoting in full from this section
of her book:

> There are at least two known monsters of the deep
> who could easily have swallowed Jonah. They are
> the Balaenoptera Musculus or sulphur-bottom
> whale, and the Rhinodon Typicus or whale shark.
> Neither of these monsters of the deep has any
> teeth. They feed in an interesting way by opening
> their enormous mouths, submerging their lower
> jaw, and rushing through the water at terrific
> speed. After straining out the water, they swallow
> whatever is left. A sulphur-bottom whale, one
> hundred feet long, was captured off Cape Cod in
> 1933. His mouth was ten or twelve feet wide—so
> big he could easily have swallowed a horse. These
> whales have four to six compartments in their
> stomachs, in any one of which a colony of men
> could find free lodging. They might even have a
> choice of rooms, for in the head of this whale is a
> wonderful air storage chamber, an enlargement of
> nasal sinus, often measuring seven feet high,
> seven feet wide, by fourteen feet long. If he has an
> unwelcome guest on board who gives him a
> headache, the whale swims to the nearest land
> and gets rid of the offender as he did Jonah.
>
> The *Cleveland Plain Dealer* recently quoted an
> article by Dr. Ransom Harvey who said that a dog
> was lost overboard from a ship. It was found in the
> head of a whale six days later, alive and barking.

Frank Bullen, F.R.G.S., who wrote, The Cruise of the Cathalot, tells of a shark fifteen feet in length which was found in the stomach of a whale. He says that when dying the whale ejects the contents of its stomach.

The late Dr. Dixon stated that in a museum at Beirut, Lebanon, there is a head of a whale shark big enough to swallow the largest man that history records! He also tells of a white shark of the Mediterranean which swallowed a whole horse; another swallowed a reindeer minus only its horns. In still another Mediterranean white shark was found a whole sea cow, about the size of an ox.

These facts show that Jonah could have been swallowed by either a whale or a shark. But has any other man besides Jonah been swallowed and lived to tell the tale? We know of two such instances.

The famous French scientist, Msr. de Parville, writes of James Bartley, who in the region of the Falkland Islands near South America, was supposed to have drowned at sea. Two days after his disappearance, the sailors made a catch of a whale. When it was cut up, much to their surprise they found their missing friend alive but unconscious inside the whale. He revived and has been enjoying the best of health ever since his adventure.

Another version of the James Bartley experience has been recorded in *The Old Farmers Almanac*, 1971 edition:

We were recently reminded of the true story of a man SWALLOWED by a whale who lived to tell about it! It concerns one James Bartley, a crewman aboard The Star of the East, a whaling ship off the Falkland Islands in February of 1891. Bartley was a member of the boat crew that was overturned by a large bull whale already wounded by a harpoon thrust. When another boat picked up the survivors, Bartley and one other man were missing. Later that afternoon, two other boats saw the same whale, captured it and drew it alongside. The Star of the East Captain, Mike Dolan, describes what then took place:

"With lines around its stomach, the crew hoisted the whale to the deck of the ship. Something moved inside the covering. Working feverishly with sharp knives, they quickly slit the stomach of the whale open and found James Bartley quivering and unconscious.

"Dashing salt water over the still form of Bartley they seemed to revive him. After he had been washed and a few sips of brandy forced through his pale lips, he was carried to the ship's cabin.

"For two weeks he hovered near death. When he finally recovered, he told a weird tale.

"Remembering being dashed high in the air when the giant whale struck the boat with his tail, Bartley said he heard a rumbling sound like a train roaring over a bridge. He imagined the noise was caused by the whale pounding the sea. In the darkness he said he made an effort to reach out and his hand touched a slick substance which yielded to his feeble efforts to escape. Then he felt himself being drawn forward into a chamber where there was more air.

"Each time he tried to crawl forward in the black chamber some invisible force seemed to draw him back. Then his terrible plight dawned upon him. He was inside the body of a whale. The heat was terrific. Weak from the strain and the heat, he sank into oblivion. Death seemed dreadfully near. He collapsed and remembered nothing until he awakened in the ship's cabin. And although his skin never quite regained its natural color, he regained his strength and lived for many years, continuing to fish in the dangerous waters where he almost met his doom."

So, was Jonah alive or dead inside the fish?

Then Jonah prayed to the Lord his God from the fish's belly.
(Jonah 2:1)

I know, somebody is going to say, "Preacher, your theory is upset already; it has gone by the board because the Bible says that Jonah prayed to the Lord inside the fish's belly." Well, my question is, when did he pray? Did he pray on the third day? Maybe he said, "Now I'm in a tight place. I've got to figure on a way of getting out of here. The thing for me to do is to pray about this. I want to pray the right kind of prayer, so I'll have to give it some thought." So he composed a prayer, then prayed it on the third day. Now may I say, if that's the way it happened, I admit my theory is no good at all, because that means he was alive if he prayed this on the third day. But I don't think he waited until the third day, do you? When would you have prayed if you had been swallowed by the fish? May I say to you, before I got through the gullet of that fish and dropped into his tummy, I would not only have prayed the prayer, but I would have covered the Book of Jonah, something you can do in three minutes. My friend, Jonah prayed this *before* he lost consciousness. "Then Jonah prayed to the LORD his God from the fish's belly."

I have a friend who was for years pastor of the First Presbyterian Church in Summerville, Tennessee. His index finger had been cut off, and it was nothing more than a stub below the second joint. When anyone would ask him about his call to the ministry, he would hold up that little stub and wave it. Then he would explain what he meant. "Well," he'd say, "I'll tell you. . . ." Then he would tell the story of his call to the ministry.

His father was an elder in the Westminster Presbyterian Church in Memphis. They were having evangelistic meetings in the church, and to obey his dad he would go every night and sit on the second row. He said, "That evangelist was getting to me, and I knew if I stayed another night I would accept Christ as my Savior. I also knew that if I did accept Christ as my Savior I would go into the ministry, and at that time I did not want to. So after everybody in the family had retired for the night, I put my extra shirt under my arm, slid down the rain gutter from my upstairs bedroom, and headed for Mississippi." He found work in a sawmill down there, and his job was to take these great logs and run them on the conveyor to the saw. If you have seen an old-time sawmill, you know how they'd do that.

One day they ran out of good logs. They had some put aside that were knotty; in fact, some of them had already been to the saw, and it had ripped them partly through before they were found to be inferior and the process reversed. It was decided, since they didn't have good logs, that they'd run these through as second class or third class lumber. He was rolling one of these logs that had been ripped almost through, and just as he let it drop onto the conveyor belt his index finger caught in the gash. The gash snapped shut, and it held him. He found himself being pulled toward that great band saw. He said, "I yelled at the top of my voice, but by that time the other end of the log had hit the saw, and no one could hear me. There I was—helpless. Between there and that saw, I covered my entire life. I prayed to the Lord and asked him for forgiveness for every sin I'd ever committed. I accepted Him as Savior; I agreed to go in the ministry; I made any other promises that the Lord wanted me to make. Since it takes only 45 seconds for a log to go through, I did all of that in 45 seconds!"

When you get in trouble it's amazing the amount of ground you can cover! He said that when the saw got to the place where his finger was, it cut off his finger. That released him, and he rolled to the side. "I hit the ground running. I did go by the doctor's office, but then I didn't stop running until I got back home and told my dad what I'd done. And I started studying for the ministry. *That* was my call to the ministry."

My friend, don't you know that Jonah prayed his prayer the minute he went inside that fish? Then he lapsed, I'm sure, into unconsciousness and then death. And God raised him from the dead. He was dead inside the fish; he didn't spend a weekend in a comfortable motel. This man spent time in the tummy of a fish, being churned up and down. He says, "Weeds were around my head." He's not trying to tell you he was alive at all! He says

. . . The earth with its bars closed behind me forever; yet You have brought up my life from the pit, O LORD, my God.
(Jonah 2:6)

The important thing for you and me to recognize is that this explanation gives young people a tool to defend the Word of God against godless professors in many of our schools.

The first time I took the position that Jonah died and was resurrected, I was a seminary student serving at the Westminster Presbyterian Church in Atlanta, Georgia, as the interim pastor before Peter Marshall came there and had his first famous pastorate. As a student, I was frightened to begin with, and for the first evening service I spoke on the Book of Jonah for the great company of young people who were there. God blessed, and several of them accepted the Lord. On my second Sunday night I was standing in the back when a young fellow came up to me and said, "Mr. McGee, I'm a student over at Georgia Tech. I'd like to accept Christ, but to be honest with you I have trouble with the Book of Jonah."

"What's your trouble?"

"Well, I have a professor who teaches mathematics, but he never misses an opportunity to ridicule the Book of Jonah. He always talks about 'that man who lived for three days inside the fish.' And I have trouble with it. How could a man live for three days inside a fish?" And I asked him, "Who told you the man lived inside that fish?"

"Well," he says, "I've heard preachers say it."

"I know, but what does the Bible say?"

"Doesn't the Bible say it?"

"Mine doesn't say it." And so we opened the Bible right there, and I went over it with that young man. He said, "Boy, wait until I get back to class!" And that young fellow accepted the Lord. When I saw him the next Sunday I asked, "How did it work out?"

"Well, my professor *always* mentioned Jonah, but we had a class Monday morning, and he didn't mention Jonah. We had a class Wednesday morning, again he didn't mention him; and I thought I was sunk, because I wanted him to mention it. So Friday morning, here he came. He said, 'Now about that fellow that lived for three days inside of a fish,' and the class laughed.

So this young fellow said to him, "Doctor, who told you the man was alive three days and three nights inside of a fish?"

He fumbled for a moment, "I've heard preachers say it."

"Yes, but what does the Bible say?"

"Well, I think the Bible says it. We'll get one."

When they finally located one, the student went over it with him, and the professor said, "Well, this is certainly a new approach, and I don't have an answer for it."

Friend, you may have been brought up to believe

that Jonah was alive all that time, and if you want to believe it that way, go ahead. But for goodness sake, give some of these young people an anchor to use in these godless schools. Back there in Georgia that professor said to the student, "Oh! Then Jonah was raised from the dead!" He answered, "Yes, and so was Jesus. And if you have trouble with one, you'll have trouble with the other."

> **For as Jonah was three days and three nights in the belly of the great fish, so will the Son of Man be three days and three nights in the heart of the earth.**
> (Matthew 12:40)

Was Jonah alive or dead?

Jonah: Dead or Alive? Part 3

GOD OF THE SECOND CHANCE

Now I want to write Luke 11:30 over this section:

> **For as Jonah became a sign to the Ninevites, so also the Son of Man will be to this generation.**

Jonah was a sign to the Ninevites. When this man arrived in the city of Nineveh, he not only *had* a message, he *was* a message. He was a sign to the Ninevites.

And that is something to keep in mind as we get into this third chapter of the Book of Jonah.

We read here in the first verse, "Now the word of the LORD came to Jonah the second time. . . ." I know some folk who consider this verse their favorite verse in the Bible. You may wonder why this could be the favorite verse of anyone. Suppose our government had commissioned a man, for instance a general, to carry a message, and he disobeyed as Jonah did. What would be done with him? They would dismiss him, wouldn't they? Would they trust him with orders a second time? I don't think so. I asked a friend of mine who was one of the vice presidents of the Bank of America in San Francisco, "Harry, if you had a cashier in one of these thousand and one branches you have, and he absconded with all the funds and then returned after spending the money down in Mexico, would you take him back and give him another chance?" He said, "Absolutely not! He had his chance. We would never give that man another chance—never again trust him with any money." I do not know, but I have a notion that would be the policy of every corporation in this country. And I'm sure many churches would never give a man a second chance. Aren't you glad, beloved, that *God* will give you a second chance? "The word of the LORD came to Jonah the second time." It's wonderful, isn't it! God gave him a second chance.

A schoolteacher spoke to me when I was teaching the Book of Jonah at Mt. Hermon. Teachers always have had the faculty of asking me questions I couldn't answer! On this particular morning she came with this question: "Dr. McGee, suppose Jonah had bought a

ticket again for Tarshish and started out, what then?"
Well, I had never thought of that, so I said to the lady,
"The only thing I can think of is that there would be
another fish out there waiting for him—or maybe the
same one. I'm confident that this man is going to Nineveh. 'The word of the LORD came to Jonah the second
time,' and since he is God's man, I don't think it will be
necessary for it to come to him the third time."

In a parallel situation, I have never read of the prodi-
gal son asking his dad to stake him the second time or
the third time to go out into the far country. He had
one fling and that was it, because he was a son of the
father. And Jonah, this backsliding prophet, is now on
the way to Nineveh, I can assure you of that. And he is
going there to give God's message. "The word of the
LORD came to Jonah the second time."

I like to think of our God as the God of the second
chance. *He* gives us a second chance. And, by the way,
He gives us more than two. I'm working somewhere up
in the hundreds. I do not know exactly where, but I'm
working way up there. God has been so gracious to me!
He gives us many chances, and He has always done
that. For instance, you may remember Jacob in the
Book of Genesis. God had made wonderful promises to
that man, yet he failed God again and again. But God
would not let him go. And one night at the Brook Jab-
bok, God crippled his leg to get him. God would not
give him up. He is the God of the second chance.

And then David, the sweet psalmist of Israel, committed an awful sin. And I do not know why, but over
the years I've noticed the soapbox orators, whom I've
heard as I have walked through the park, are usually

preaching on David. They feel like God made a terrible blunder choosing David and letting him have a second chance. Without question the double sin he committed was awful. The Bible doesn't tone it down. But aren't you glad God gave him a second chance? If He had not, we wouldn't have Psalm 23; we wouldn't have Psalm 32; we wouldn't have Psalm 51; and we wouldn't have almost a hundred other psalms, for David wrote most of these psalms following that experience. And you don't read about David continuing to live in disobedience to God. David slipped, and God gave him a second chance. He is the God of the second chance.

And then Simon Peter, you remember, stumbled and fell. And our Lord had even warned him,

". . . Simon, Simon! Indeed, Satan has asked for you, that he may sift you as wheat. But I have prayed for you, that your faith should not fail. . . ."
(Luke 22:31–32)

God says, "I'll not give you up." And this man Simon Peter was given the privilege of preaching the first sermon on the Day of Pentecost when 3,000 men came to Christ. And God gave him a wonderful lifelong ministry. God did not give him up.

Also, John Mark is an example in the Scriptures of one who failed. He was on the first missionary journey with Paul and his uncle Barnabas, whose name means "son of consolation." But when John Mark looked out on that frightful wilderness of Asia Minor, he showed a yellow streak down his back, and he headed home to mama. So when they were ready for the second journey, Barnabas said, "Let's take John Mark with us again and give him another chance." In effect, Paul's response was, "Absolutely not! Do you think I would take a man who had so failed on the first missionary journey? I won't give him another chance." But Uncle Barnabas took him anyway. The team of Paul and Barnabas split over John Mark because Paul wouldn't have him. But Paul was proven wrong. And there came the day when Paul acknowledged it—in fact, in his swan song he wrote, ". . . Get Mark and bring him with you, for he is useful to me for ministry" (2 Timothy 4:11). Isn't that a wonderful thing—John Mark made good! God didn't give him up after his first failure. God gave him another chance.

After giving these messages on Jonah on a radio program in downtown Los Angeles many years ago, I received a letter from a doctor in Beverly Hills. He wrote: "Thank God for Jonah 3:1. That now is my favorite verse, and I'll tell you why." Then he told me his experience. He had been an officer in a church in Chicago, and some problem had arisen. Charges had been brought against him. He said he was not guilty at all, but everyone turned against him. He found no sympathy, no understanding from anyone in the church. So he walked out. He even moved his practice to Southern California and became a success out here, but he would never darken the door of a church. He said, "Never again!"

However he did listen to our radio program. And, friend, may I say to you, that has been the wonder of radio. We never know who is listening. We find that there are countless numbers of people who have never darkened the door of anyone's church, but they will listen to the radio. And that doctor was listening the night we came to this third chapter of Jonah. He said, "If God would give those men a second chance, He will give me a second chance." And this man came back to the Lord. So as a preacher I wrote a very professional letter and urged him to become active in some church, and he wrote back: "I've already done that!" May I say to you, the word of the Lord came to this doctor in our contemporary society the second time; and there are any number of people to whom the word of the Lord has come the second time, giving them a second chance. Only God will do that. And God will give you and me a second chance.

Putting It on the Line

So let's follow this man Jonah as God gives him a second chance and sends him into the city of Nineveh. We're told, "So the LORD spoke to the fish, and it vomited Jonah onto dry land" (Jonah 2:10). At last he is out on the dry land, and we believe God has raised him from the dead.

Now the word of the LORD came to Jonah the second time, saying, "Arise, go to Nineveh, that great city, and preach to it the message that I tell you."
(Jonah 3:1–2)

And this man now will give one of the most startling messages that city ever heard.

So Jonah arose and went to Nineveh, according to the word of the LORD. Now

Nineveh was an exceedingly great city, a three-day journey in extent.
(Jonah 3:3)

Now if you were to go back to the nineteenth century, you would find writers of the school of higher criticism ridiculing this story, not just on account of the fish, but on account of the statements attributed to the Lord that Nineveh was a great city; and Jonah says it was an *exceedingly* great city! An ancient city of that size just wasn't possible at all, according to the critics, because anyone knows that the ancient cities—certainly one as prominent as Nineveh—would have had walls around them. Even Babylon in all of its glory was not a great city in size. It was compressed together, with very narrow streets, so that in time of a siege people could get inside of it. Babylon was walled in, and that had to be true of Nineveh, the critics reasoned; and in their view, by no means could it be said that it was an *exceedingly* great city.

Well, that was before Sir Austen Layard, the French archaeologist, and others with him were in Mosul. They could see across the Tigris River a very large tell or mound two and one-half miles long in the shape of a trapezium. These men began to make inquiry of the natives there and came to the conclusion it must be ancient Nineveh. When they began to excavate, they found that it was, indeed, the ancient city of Nineveh. But even with that discovery, the size didn't meet the measurements necessary for what Jonah was saying. So these men probed further and found there was a tremendous valley there, a valley that was filled not with just one city but quite a few of them; and three of them were prominent cities. You see, Nineveh was located at a juncture of the Tigris River and the upper Zab. It was the city farthest to the north. About twenty miles south of Nineveh, at another juncture of the upper Zab and the Tigris River, was the city of Calah. Then on the upper Zab and about ten miles east of Nineveh was the city of Khorsabad. Now there were other cities also in this area. It was low, rich land—in the South we would call it bottom land—which was easily farmed. And so this was a very rich and apparently irrigated area. It was the center of a tremendous population.

There's a very interesting passage in the Bible, way back in Genesis 10:11–12, which speaks of this particular area:

From that land he [Nimrod] went to Assyria and built Nineveh, Rehoboth Ir, Calah, and Resen between Nineveh and Calah (that is the principal city).

So we know now that Nineveh was a tremendous area by all standards. Even by today's standard it would be considered very large. Obviously, the man who wrote the Book of Jonah was an eyewitness. He had been there!

Frankly, I think it would correspond to the Los Angeles basin in many ways. They had natural fortifications with the Tigris River on the west, and on the south and to the east the Zab River; plus, there was a wall. As a result, this entire area could be protected from an enemy and was protected for many centuries. It was actually a flood of the Tigris River which took out a portion of the wall that finally permitted an enemy to come in and destroy this city. Nineveh was an exceedingly great city.

Now we are told here that Jonah entered the city:

And Jonah began to enter the city on the first day's walk. Then he cried out and said, "Yet forty days, and Nineveh shall be overthrown!"
(Jonah 3:4)

This man comes into the city with this very startling message, a message that would shock the people. His only problem was, how would he get a crowd? He was not known in the city of Nineveh. The king didn't know him; none of the great people in Nineveh knew him, nor was there a committee to arrange for a campaign. So how did Jonah get a crowd? If you were a preacher you would worry about this. It would be of great concern to you, especially in these days of apostasy. How would a prophet of God, going into the pagan city of Nineveh, get a crowd?

Well, let me call you back now to this man Jonah who had spent three days inside a fish with the gastric juices working upon the epidermis of this backsliding prophet. I can tell you that he was a mess when he came out of that fish!

I have given one account of a man being swallowed by a fish near the Falkland Islands. But, let me briefly give you another. Dr. Harry Rimmer, President of the

Research Science Bureau in Los Angeles, writes of another case. "In *Literary Digest* we noticed an account of an English sailor who was swallowed by a gigantic Rhinoden in the English Channel. Briefly, the account stated that in an attempt to harpoon one of these monstrous sharks the man fell overboard, before he could be picked up again, the shark turned and engulfed him. Forty-eight hours after the accident occurred, the fish was sighted and slain. When the shark was opened by the sailors, they were amazed to find the man unconscious but alive! He was rushed to the hospital where he was found to be suffering from shock, and a few hours later was discharged as being physically fit."

Dr. Rimmer was in London, England, two years after that, and this man was being advertised as the Jonah of the twentieth century. When Dr. Rimmer went to see him, he noticed that he was very strange, in fact, startling looking! He didn't have a hair on his body, and his head looked like a billiard ball. His skin was covered with patches of a very peculiar yellowish brown color. Dr. Rimmer said you would notice him anywhere he'd go, and that was two years after he had been inside the fish.

Now Jonah spent three days inside a fish. (We don't think he was alive, but that's beside the point right at this moment.) Inside that fish the gastric juices had been working on him for three days and three nights, and now this man has come into the city. I want to tell you, he was a sight to see! And our Lord makes it very clear. He says, "As Jonah became a sign to the Ninevites . . ." (Luke 11:30). I think when this man came to a street corner and stopped to wait for a street light, the people gathered around him and said, "Brother, where have you been?" And it didn't take him long to gather a crowd. He probably said to them, "I'm a man who has come back from the dead to bring you a message from God."

"You don't mean it!"

"I certainly do, and I'll tell you my experience." And he'd give them his experience, then say, "I'm back here to tell you that in forty days this city is to be destroyed." May I say to you, the entire population of that city began to listen to this strange-looking man.

Now let's get this down to where we can get hold of it. These things are real, you know. I think of that area where Nineveh was located as very much like Southern California where we are spreading out in every direction. Maybe that's true in your city. Suppose a man began in the city center and walked from corner to corner all the way to the outskirts. Don't you think that by the time he had gotten halfway the word would have spread until everybody was coming to hear what he had to say? Obviously this man Jonah was a sensation in the city of Nineveh! And our Lord says he was a *sign* to these Ninevites.

When God Relents

Jonah began to enter the city—a day's journey. He cried out with a startling message, "Yet forty days, and Nineveh shall be overthrown!" But even more startling than the message, more sensational than the fish or anything else in the story, is the reaction of the people.

So the people of Nineveh believed God, . . .
(Jonah 3:5)

And I want to say to you, friend, had I been the head of a mission board sending out missionaries in that day and somebody said to me, "Why don't you send one of your missionaries into Nineveh?" I would have said, "Let's forget that place. That's a godless city. They are the most brutal people in the world. There's no use sending a missionary there. It wouldn't do a bit of good!" I don't know but what you might say the same thing. You would look at the brutality and sin in that city and say it's hopeless. God didn't think so. God wanted a message brought to this city. And all it says here is that the people of Nineveh believed God.

Now think this over very carefully. Did you know that all God has ever asked any person to do is to believe Him? That's all. It's amazing today how easy it is to believe *people*. While we were away recently, we heard a rumor that our organist at the church had broken her arm on Thursday night. I told everybody she had broken her arm, because that's what I had been told. I just believed them. Then on Sunday morning, much to my chagrin, there she sat, playing the organ as usual. You may think I'm gullible anyway, and maybe I am; but I believed what I heard. Isn't it interesting that we readily believe what people say and yet find it difficult to believe what God says? "If we receive the witness of men, the witness of God is greater. . . ." (1 John 5:9). But these godless, brutal people of Nineveh believed God!

My friend, all that God ever asked any of us to

believe is that He gave His Son to die on the cross for us; and if we will receive Him, God says, "I'll save you." All God asks a sinner to do is just to *believe* Him! And we're told that the people of Nineveh believed God. Someone says, "They were terrible people!" They sure were, and Jonah believed that for a long time, too, as we'll see in chapter 4 when we get to it.

So the people of Nineveh believed God, proclaimed a fast, and put on sackcloth, from the greatest to the least of them. Then word came to the king of Nineveh; . . .

And this is amazing!

. . . and he arose from his throne and laid aside his robe, covered himself with sackcloth and sat in ashes. And he caused it to be proclaimed and published throughout Nineveh by the decree of the king and his nobles, saying, "Let neither man nor beast, herd nor flock, taste anything; do not let them eat, or drink water."

All the way from the king on the throne to the peasant in the hovel, this entire city turned to God!

"But let man and beast be covered with sackcloth, and cry mightily to God; yes, let every one turn from his evil way and from the violence that is in his hands."
(Jonah 3:5–8)

And this city was noted for its violence! Nineveh was hated throughout the world, probably more hated than any other nation in its day; but everyone turned from his violence and from his brutality. These people turned *to* God, and when they did, they turned *from* their evil ways.

Friend, there is nothing else like this on record anywhere. There has never been a great turning to God to equal this.

Why Nineveh?

Why did God choose this wicked city? The very interesting thing is that the examples given to us in the Scriptures are always extreme. Whom did God choose to save in the city of Jericho? He picked Rahab the harlot. I heard a man speaking on the radio the other day who sure cleaned up Rahab's character. He said she was merely an innkeeper running a motel. May I say to you, that's not what the Bible says. But God saved her, if you please. Why? Because she believed God.

And God saved the entire city of Nineveh—a brutal, pagan, heathen city—to let the Gentile world know He will save anybody who will turn to Him and believe Him. And, of course, that still holds good today.

Now the king's word went throughout Nineveh; and the entire city went into sackcloth and ashes, crying out to God for mercy because they believed God. And what did happen?

"Who can tell if God will turn and relent, and turn away from His fierce anger, so that we may not perish?" Then God saw their works, that they turned from their

evil way; and God relented from the disaster that He had said He would bring upon them, and He did not do it.
(Jonah 3:9–10)

God said He would destroy Nineveh, but He did not destroy Nineveh. The only prophecy of Jonah that we have recorded is, "Yet forty days, and Nineveh shall be overthrown!" But it wasn't overthrown. God did not destroy Nineveh. So, did Jonah give a wrong prophecy? No, it happened to be a right prophecy. Had God changed His mind? Was God wishy-washy?

Someone asked that of Dr. G. Campbell Morgan years ago in England: "Dr. Morgan, is God as changeable as a weather vane?" His reply was, "You used the wrong illustration. A weather vane is not changeable. It never changes. It operates according to a law that says it doesn't make any difference which way the wind will blow, the weather vane always points in the direction the wind is going. It is the wind that does the changing."

Who really changed? God or Nineveh? The weather vane turned to Nineveh because God will always save when people turn to Him. He *has* never changed. He *will* never change. And if they don't turn to Him, He will do what He promised—He will judge.

If you want the sequel to the story of Jonah, read the little prophecy of Nahum written a hundred years later. It is the judgment of Nineveh. By then the city had again turned from God, and this time they did not repent of it. The revival was gone. Judgment came, and Nineveh was left in ruins. Even the ruins were lost to civilization until the city was excavated in the nine-teenth century. May I say to you, God never changes.

It does not matter which way the wind is blowing in your life, God never changes. He will save any sinner who will come to Him in faith. The writer to the Hebrews assures us that,

Jesus Christ is the same yesterday, today, and forever.
(Hebrews 13:8)

Jonah: Dead or Alive?
Part 4

TO THE HEART OF GOD

Jonah had a most remarkable experience; he experienced what no other man ever has from the very beginning. From Noah's preaching down to the preaching of Billy Graham, no one has ever seen one hundred percent saturation of the Word of God bring one hundred percent conversion; but this man saw it. Jonah had the experience of seeing an entire city turn to God!

Jonah Is Displeased

Now if you and I had that experience, I think we would go down to Western Union and send a wire back to Jerusalem: "Rejoice with me. The revival is here! It's broken out in the city of Nineveh!" You'd think that Jonah would have done something like this. But no! Chapter 4 opens with a startling statement. This, to me, is the strangest part of the Book of Jonah:

But it displeased Jonah exceedingly, and he became angry.
(Jonah 4:1)

Now God has more problems with this backsliding prophet than He had with the entire population of Nineveh! When this man declared the message, "Yet forty days, and Nineveh shall be overthrown!" the people of Nineveh believed God. Do you know that all God has ever asked sinners to do is to *believe* what He has done for them? They need to know that He is a God of judgment but that He also is a God of mercy. Paul, when he reasoned with Felix, spoke with him about the mercy of God and the saving power of Jesus Christ, but he also reasoned with him about judgment. And, my friend, lost men and women today are moving to a frightful judgment without Jesus Christ!

And so this city of Nineveh believed God, and they turned to God; and this man Jonah was displeased by it! Now why was he displeased? If I had been in Jonah's shoes, and if I had been in Jonah's fish, I might have felt the same way he did. This Scripture will give us some insight into the heart of Jonah.

So he prayed to the LORD, and said, "Ah, LORD, was not this what I said when I was still in my country? Therefore I fled previously to Tarshish . . . .

There have been commentators who said the reason Jonah acted as he did is that he really didn't know God.

But Jonah makes it clear the problem is that he *did* know God. Listen to him:

> **. . . for I know that You are a gracious and merciful God, slow to anger and abundant in lovingkindness, One who relents from doing harm.**
> (Jonah 4:2)

Oh, my friend, you and I haven't any conception of how gracious and merciful our God is and how He longs to save. But, you see, He is a holy God, and He has made one way for a man to be saved. The apostle Peter in speaking of Jesus said,

> **. . . there is no other name under heaven given among men by which we must be saved.**
> (Acts 4:12)

This is the message that must be gotten out if folk are to experience the mercy of God and know something of the grace of God; because, my friend, apart from Jesus Christ a frightful, awful eternity is before every individual. And it would be before us today if Christ had not borne that judgment death for us upon the cross.

Notice that Jonah says, "You are a gracious and merciful God, slow to anger and abundant in lovingkindness, One who relents from doing harm." In other words, when God called him to go to Nineveh and speak to that city and tell them that because of their wickedness God would destroy them, Jonah knew what would happen.

The Ninevites were evil people. You talk about violence and lawlessness! This city was given over to it. It was dreaded and feared in the ancient world. When the Assyrian army moved against a city, sometimes an entire population in a community would commit suicide rather than fall into the hands of those brutal Assyrians. Jonah knew God was merciful and that actually God would save even Ninevites. And Jonah says in effect, "Those rascals, I don't trust them. They might say they've turned to God, and then not do it. Or they might sincerely turn to God, and if they did, God would save them." He knew what God would do, and he did not want the Ninevites saved, so he headed in the opposite direction. But then God gave him a second chance to do His will, detouring him around and sending him to Nineveh despite his mind-set.

Now, having done his assignment, listen to this man. He concludes his prayer by saying,

> **Therefore now, O LORD, please take my life from me, for it is better for me to die than to live!**
> (Jonah 4:3)

Jonah wants to die. May I say to you, I think he's the most miserable person on topside of the earth at this time. Actually, the most miserable people in the world are Christians out of the will of God. Dwight L. Moody, in his quaint way, used to put it like this: "Some people have just enough religion to make them miserable."

And other people may actually be saved, but are certainly not enjoying the ride to heaven. Neither are they being used of God. I won't question Jonah's salvation, because he is God's man. But, again, God had more trouble with this backsliding prophet than He did with the entire city of Nineveh. And God was going to work on Jonah. He was God's prophet, and he did deliver His message to the Ninevites.

Now will you notice God's method. I think it still may be His method "for He knows our frame; He remembers that we are dust" (Psalm 103:14). God knows us. And He knew Jonah. In other words, God is a very good psychiatrist without having read any of the modern books! God understands human nature, especially fallen human nature. He understands this old nature that you and I inherited from Adam when he rebelled against God.

Listen to the Lord's response to Jonah:

Then the Lord said, "Is it right for you to be angry?"
(Jonah 4:4)

In my judgment Dr. G. Douglas Young has the best translation here: "Is doing good displeasing to thee?" Jonah says, "I want to die." And the fact of the matter is, I suppose that most of us at one time or another have said, "I wish I were dead," and we didn't mean it at all. We said it because we were miserable or some difficulty had come into our life. But nobody, as far as I know, ever died by wishing. You're safe when you say that; it's not incurable by any means. So Jonah says,

"It's better for me to die than to live." And God says to him, "Is it right for you to be angry?" In other words, "Look, Jonah, you have to admit that I have done good. Whether you like Ninevites or not, I've done good. You will have to admit that is true because I have saved these Ninevites."

"So Jonah went out of the city . . . ." He's in a huff now; he doesn't like what God said to him. He's out of fellowship with God; and you can be sure of one thing, he doesn't have a friend in the city of Nineveh. His hometown is several hundred miles away, and he is homesick, and he is lonely. This is the time when God is going to move in on this man.

So Jonah went out of the city and sat on the east side of the city. There he made himself a shelter. . . .
(Jonah 4:5)

Today you'd liken it to a trailer court, I suppose, but actually he made only a camp out there, just a booth or shelter to live in. We know the topography of the land where Nineveh and Calah and Khorsabad were, the three great cities in that valley. It was very extensive and supported a great population, and the land was all irrigated. I think Jonah went up on the hill, which was the protection for the city, where he could get a seat on the fifty-yard line to see if the Ninevites were really sincere in their repentance. Jonah didn't trust them. He did not believe they were genuine.

It is very interesting to compare the little prophecy of Nahum with the Book of Jonah. We read there that several generations later Nineveh had turned away from God and had lapsed back into idolatry. And when you read Nahum, you find God destroyed the city of Nineveh at that time. And, as we mentioned in Part 3, it was lost to mankind and to history until 1860 when Layard, the French archaeologist, saw that tell across from Mosul on the Tigris River and began to excavate. And he found out it was, as he suspected, the ruins of the ancient city of Nineveh. The first thing that had happened to cause its destruction was a flood that took out one corner of the wall. This let the enemy in, and the city fell to its enemies. But that did not happen until 100 or 150 years after Jonah's day.

Now under Jonah's preaching, the Ninevites have turned to God, and God has saved them. But this man Jonah wants to get a good seat up at an elevation where he can look out over the city, intending to stay there until the fire falls from heaven, because he doesn't believe they are sincere. And Jonah knows God. He knows He is merciful and that He will save these Ninevites. However, if they are not genuine, he knows God will judge them. And Jonah is so sure they will go back to their old sins, he is out there waiting.

God Is Gracious

There sits this lonely, backsliding prophet, so unhappy he'd like to die.

So Jonah went out of the city and sat on the east side of the city. There he made himself a shelter and sat under it in the shade, till he might see what would

become of the city. And the LORD God pre-pared a plant [in some versions called a gourd] **and made it come up over Jonah, that it might be shade for his head to deliver him from his misery. So Jonah was very grateful for the plant.**
(Jonah 4:5–6)

This plant, this gourd vine, is as miraculous as the fish. The record tells us that the fish was prepared, and the gourd also was prepared. One is just as miraculous as the other. Now, friend, Jonah he got attached to that little gourd plant. You see, it was God who made this gourd sprout up and grow. Jonah hasn't had anything living that he can communicate with, and we are so made that even if we are not gregarious creatures, we want to communicate with somebody or something.

It's amazing how we can get attached to a living thing. I was speaking some years ago at the Moody Founder's Week Conference in Chicago, and some friends invited me out to dinner. As soon as I got inside their apartment the lady of the house wanted to show me her geranium. She said, "I know you come from the place where they grow geraniums, but I want you to see mine." So I went with her, and all I saw was a little stalk sticking out of a flower pot. That's all it was. There wasn't even a bloom on the thing! She said to me, "Isn't it nice?" And she petted the flowerpot and began to *talk* to the plant. She's a sane woman, I can assure you of that, a very wonderful Christian! But she actually talked to that little green stub and said, "Dr. McGee grows geraniums in California." And, friend, I want to tell you that if that geranium had spoken back, she and I both would have jumped out the window of that apartment. But she was attached to it, and I found out that you can get attached to living things like that.

For many years I was really rough on owners of dogs. But I've learned to appreciate dog owners. I'm attached to a dog now, and I'm not saying anything ugly about dog owners anymore. My daughter brought the dog home one night, a big husky, the biggest dog I'd ever seen. I asked her when she came in with him, "Did you bring a saddle?" And I thought, *My, we can't keep this dog*. And then there came along a young fellow who married my daughter and took her all the way across the country. When she left she said to me, "Now I'll leave the dog with you." Well, the dog misses her, and I miss her. The fact of the matter is, the dog and I sit on the patio, do you know what? I *talk* to the dog! My wife came to the door the other day and said, "Who are you talking to out here?" I said, "I'm talking to the smartest dog in the world." He and I take walks up one of those trails in the foothills of the San Gabriel mountains, and I talk to him. One time we met a fellow on the trail, and he looked around to see who was with me. He sure seemed glad to get on down the trail, I'll tell you that! It's amazing how you can get attached to a living plant or animal.

Jonah became attached to the gourd. I imagine Jonah got a bucket that very day and went down to the Tigris River, filled the bucket with water, came back, and poured the water around the roots of the gourd and started to train the vine to grow up over his booth that he'd made. And I think he talked to it. "Oh, you're running the wrong way, little gourd." And, of course, Jonah had been running the wrong way too; and he was still running the wrong way. But he says to the vine, "I'll have to train you this way." Believe me, he got attached very quickly to the only living thing he could talk to. And God had arranged all this purposely. Watch how He is going to move in on Jonah:

> **But as morning dawned the next day God prepared a worm, and it so damaged the plant that it withered.**
> (Jonah 4:7)

"But God prepared a worm. . . ." This worm is just as miraculous as the fish. ". . . And it so damaged the plant that it withered." This worm cut the vine down because worms just don't fall in love with vines—they would rather eat them.

> **And it happened, when the sun arose, that God prepared a vehement east wind; and the sun beat on Jonah's head, so that he grew faint. Then he wished death for himself, and said, "It is better for me to die than to live."**
> (Jonah 4:8)

Here he goes again, *wishing;* but it won't do him a bit of good.

We have had here in the Book of Jonah a prepared fish, a prepared gourd, a prepared worm, and a prepared vehement east wind. All of them are miraculous—each one of them—and they are equally miraculous. The vehement east wind was just as miraculous as the fish was. You see, God is dealing with this man. Jonah has lost his gourd vine, the little living thing to which he had become attached. It's dead now, and he's actually grieving over it because it's the only living thing he had. You say such behavior is ridiculous! May I say to you, it's ridiculous the gourds that you and I get attached to in this world today. How many people have a "gourd" to which they are giving their time, giving their energy, giving their money, giving everything—and what is it really?

Heart to Heart

Listen now to God as He speaks to Jonah:

Then God said to Jonah, "Is it right for you to be angry about the plant?"

Then notice Jonah's answer:

. . . And he said, "It is right for me to be angry, even to death!"
(Jonah 4:9)

In other words, Jonah says, "This is it! I want to die. You didn't destroy Nineveh, but you did destroy my gourd!" He's a petulant little prophet, isn't he? He's an unhappy prophet. He's a miserable prophet. And he's like a lot of the critical saints today. They've got a gourd, and they don't want anybody to take the gourd away from them. How did the Lord respond?

But the LORD said, "You have had pity on the plant for which you have not labored,

nor made it grow, which came up in a night and perished in a night."
(Jonah 4:10)

God is showing this man how ridiculous it is. He says to Jonah, "Jonah, a gourd is nothing." My friend, I hate to say this, but a pussycat is nothing, a little dog is nothing; but a human being has a soul that is either going to heaven or hell. And God did not ask you to *love* the lost before you go to them. He said, "*I* love the lost, and I want you to go to them." That is what He is saying to Jonah: "Jonah, I love the Ninevites."

And should I not pity Nineveh, that great city, in which are more than one hundred and twenty thousand persons who cannot discern between their right hand and their left—and much livestock?
(Jonah 4:11)

Who does He mean by "one hundred and twenty thousand persons who cannot discern between their right hand and their left"? He means little children. God says, "You wouldn't want Me to destroy that city, would you, Jonah? If you can fall in love with a gourd vine, can't you at least fall in love with Ninevite children?"

Now, may I make this application? When I was teaching in a Bible institute, I used to say (like all the other teachers were saying) that if you are called to go as a missionary, you ought to love the people to whom you go. I disagree vehemently with that now, because how can you love people before you know them? I first applied that to myself. I have never accepted a call to a church because I loved the people; I didn't know them to begin with. I went because I felt that God had called me to go there and preach. But I also have never been in a church in which I didn't become involved with the people. I have stood at their bedsides in hospitals; I've been at their gravesides when death came; I've been with them in the marriages that have taken place in their families; and I can truthfully say that I have never yet left a church where there wasn't a great company of people whom I loved—and I really mean that I *loved* them in the Lord. But I did not love them when I first went there, because I did not know them.

God is saying to a great many people today, "I want you to go and take the Word of God to those who are lost." And they say, "But I don't love them." God says, "I never asked you to love them; I asked you to *go*." I cannot find anywhere that God ever asked Jonah to go because he loved the Ninevites. He said, "Jonah, I want you to go because I love them—I love Ninevites. I want to save Ninevites. I want you to take the message to them."

Again, may I say that I am afraid there are a great many people in the church who are caterpillars. Church members are either pillars or caterpillars: The pillars hold up the church, and the caterpillars just crawl in and out. There are a lot of people just crawling in and out of the church—waiting for some great wave of emotion, waiting for some feeling to take hold of them—and they have never done anything yet. God says that we are to get busy for Him.

I remember talking to a missionary who was home from Africa, and he was showing me a picture of some little black boys in the orphans' home there. I could tell by the way he looked at the picture that he loved those little boys. I said to him, "When you first went to Africa, did you love the Africans?" He said, "No, I really wanted to go to my people in Greece, but at that time the door was closed and I could not go; so I had to go to Africa." As he held that picture, I said to him, "But do you love those little fellows now?" Tears came to his eyes. He said, "Yes, I love them now."

God says to you and me, "You go with the Word. I love the lost. You take the Word to them, and when they are saved and you get acquainted with them and know them, you will love them too."

Since Jonah wrote the book, I think it is reasonable to say that after this experience he left the dead gourd vine and went down to where the living were walking the streets of Nineveh, and I think he rejoiced with them that they had come to a saving knowledge of God. My friend, what a message this is! Why don't you get involved in getting the Word of God out to people? Don't wait to be motivated by things that are emotional. Take the Word of God to them because God loves them; and if you'll do that, I will guarantee that you will learn to love them also.

7

ZACCHAEUS

Fruit of the Sycamore Tree
Luke 19:1–8

It happened as I was driving to an industrial plant here in Southern California where I was scheduled to speak to a large group of men at a noon service, and again as I was given a brief tour of the plant—the story of Zacchaeus kept recurring in my mind. Suddenly I realized something new had penetrated my heart, and it seemed that the Lord revealed to me the purpose of this wonderful incident in the ministry of Jesus. So under the inspiration of just having received a new truth, I scrapped the message I had prepared and spoke at that noonday service on Zacchaeus. The reaction to the message and the results from it clearly indicated to me that this had, indeed, been of the Lord!

The importance of the encounter with Zacchaeus in the life of our Lord is that it affords an illustration for one of the difficult texts of Scripture, James 2:20:

But do you want to know, O foolish man, that faith without works is dead?

One of the problems of the church is reconciling the positions of Paul and James as to the place of good works in the plan of salvation. I had long felt that if a Bible illustration of this great truth was to be found, it would help identify the place of good works in the gospel of grace. The new truth which came to me that day was that Zacchaeus is the illustration for which I had been searching.

Those of us who belong to the school that emphasizes the grace of God in salvation are often reluctant to speak of good works for fear of complicating God's glorious grace. Not only does God save without the good works of man even entering into the picture, but God saves in spite of man's so-called good works. Yet we recognize that all too often the practical aspect of good works has not had its proper place.

THERE IS A MOVEMENT . . .

Now let us consider this record of Zacchaeus.

Then Jesus entered and passed through Jericho.
(Luke 19:1)

In the record of Luke there is a movement, beginning in chapter 9 when Jesus left Caesarea Philippi, which would take Him to Jerusalem and to the cross. In Luke 9:51 we read, "Now it came to pass, when the time had come for Him to be received up, that He steadfastly set His face to go to Jerusalem." Our Lord moved out of that area, through Galilee and Samaria; then He apparently crossed the Jordan River and continued down the east side until He was over against Jericho. As He entered Jericho, there was a blind man. Actually there were two blind men, but here Luke gives us the record of only one of them. There was, however, according to Luke, one blind man who encountered Jesus as He entered the city and another blind man who met Him when He was leaving the city, as we shall see.

The movement here is *through* Jericho. He entered and passed through. He never spent a night in Jericho, for it was the accursed city. This was the first city that God had given to the people of Israel when they returned to enter the promised land after forty years in the wilderness. It was the city from which nothing personal was to be salvaged, and a curse was placed on any person who would attempt to rebuild it. If you want to read the record, in 1 Kings 16:34 a man rebuilt the city and reaped the curse in all its fullness—both he and his family. Though eventually the city was rebuilt, it remained an accursed city. It was a city where there was great sin, a place where gangsters resorted. Our Lord, on the way to the cross, did not bypass Jericho but purposely went through it because there was a sinner there who needed Him, a tax collector called a publican.

This is the movement: Jesus entered and passed

through. What a picture it is of His entire mission and ministry to this world! He puts it succinctly, as recorded in John 16:28: "I came forth from the Father and have come into the world. Again, I leave the world and go to the Father." He came from heaven's glory to this sin-cursed earth, not to just an accursed city but to a *world* on which the curse of sin rests. Anywhere you look today on this earth you see the evidences and the ravages of sin. He left heaven's glory, and He came to this earth for the same purpose that He entered and passed through Jericho. He came not to get only one sinner but to get any sinner who would trust Him. At the time of this incident, Jesus was on His way to the cross to die for Zacchaeus and to die for a world of sinners. Such is the movement here.

THE MAN ZACCHAEUS

We are introduced to Zacchaeus, and the Spirit of God gives a total picture, an entire biography with one flourish of the pen. There are three things which are said about Zacchaeus. These three facts tell out his story, and what a story it is!

> **Now behold, there was a man named Zacchaeus who was a chief tax collector, and he was rich.**
> (Luke 19:2)

His Name

The first statement concerning him is that he was named Zacchaeus. The name *Zacchaeus* is from *zaccai* and means "pure." That is not a name for a publican to have! It is like saying black snow, white coal, and cold fire—the two terms are self-contradictory. A publican. Zacchaeus! But, after all, it was his parents who gave him this name. When they looked down in the crib and saw the little fellow, they said, "He is so sweet and pure there is only one name that fits him—Zacchaeus." So they named him Pure. Believe me, friends, that was some name for a man to carry around, especially after he became a tax collector or publican! In Southern California there was a famous gangster who said when he was arrested some years ago that he was "as pure as snow." The reporters for awhile tagged him "Snow White," and when they called him that, I thought of Zacchaeus. You can well imagine what delight the other publicans had in calling this man, who was an obvious sinner, Pure! He was anything but that.

Chief Among Publicans

The second feature recorded about Zacchaeus is that he was chief among the publicans. There are in the New Testament two little men who are identified as great sinners: Saul of Tarsus and Zacchaeus. Saul of Tarsus took the name Paul, which means "small." It was the name he evidently chose to speak of himself. When he was writing of his life prior to the Damascus Road experience, he said that he was "the chief of sinners." That is not an oratorical gesture nor hyperbole; Paul meant it because it was true. Jesus Christ and the church never had an enemy any worse than Saul of Tarsus; he was the *chief* of sinners. And this man Zacchaeus was a little man, but he was called the "chief tax collector." Throughout the Gospels there is the grouping together of publicans and sinners, and the interesting thing is that the publicans are always mentioned first. It is not sinners and publicans, but publicans and sinners, because publicans were the worst kind of sinners; and Zacchaeus was *chief* among the publicans. Two little men in the New Testament were chief among sinners.

A publican was a Jew who had sold out his nation. In those days the people of Israel were governed by the empire of Rome, and the Roman government had a system whereby it turned over the dirty business of collecting taxes to the natives of the countries it had captured. Instead of using roughhouse methods of collecting taxes from a captive people, they found a traitor, a quisling, someone who was willing to betray his nation for a price—a good price, by the way. A publican could buy a certain territory at a certain rate; then he could go in and collect taxes in that section at whatever rate he chose.

Being a publican meant that at one time in his life he had been faced with a decision. A similar decision comes to every man and to every woman. Each of us has to decide whether we will be honest or dishonest in business. Everyone decides whether to be pure or impure. There is no alternative. Every person is faced with that decision in this life. This man Zacchaeus came to such a crossroad. Before him there were two ways he could go. One way was probably a continuation of his monotonous life which, though honorable, would bring him no riches. The other way was to become a publican. Now if he should become a publican, it would be a one-way street; he could never come back.

No publican could come back. He would cut himself loose from his nation; and the minute he cut himself loose from his nation, which was Israel, he cut himself loose from his religion—from the temple, from the place of sacrifice, from any mercy whatsoever. In fact, he would cut himself loose from his God. It was a dark night when Zacchaeus weighed his future. "Either I continue to be honest, serving God as I was brought up to do, or else I can become a publican. I can get rich . . . it will pay me . . . I will get the things I want. But if I do that, I will cut myself off from my nation." I say it was a dark night because he made the wrong decision. He became a publican, and in time he became chief among the publicans. That means he was the biggest rascal in Jericho, and there were some big-time operators there.

A Rich Man

The third identifying word about Zacchaeus is this: "he was rich." He made his position pay.

Perhaps you are a person who feels that if you were rich all your problems would be solved. Now I can't speak from experience, but from observation I would say that the rich seem to be the most unhappy. From where do the majority of our suicides come? They come from among the upper class, the rich. Somehow they have not found satisfaction in this life. We talk of reaching the down-and-outer, but the up-and-outer is probably in worse condition because no one goes to him with the gospel. Zacchaeus was an up-and-outer.

WANTED—A MERCY SEAT

Our Lord knew Zacchaeus. You will remember that He ". . . had no need that anyone should testify of man, for He knew what was in man" (John 2:25). He knew this man. In the chapter immediately preceding the record of His encounter with Zacchaeus, our Lord gave a parable which I believe was a true incident. I do not think that our Lord ever made up a story but that they were all based on true incidents taken from life.

Jesus told of two men who went up to the temple to pray. One was a Pharisee, and the other was a publican. The publican stood afar off and beat on his breast saying, "God, be merciful to me a sinner." Why did he beat on his breast? Because he did not have access to the mercy seat. He repudiated his nation and repudiated his God when he became a publican. He was an outcast, and all he could do was stand outside the temple and cry, "God, be merciful!" Actually, he did not say exactly that. The word in the Greek is not *mercy* but *mercy seat*, that place yonder in the temple where every instructed Israelite knew blood was sprinkled, giving him access to God. In our day, Christ is that mercy seat. "And He Himself is the propitiation for our sins, and not for ours only but also for the whole world" (1 John 2:2). What this publican is saying is this: "O God, make for me, a publican, a mercy seat where I can go. I have no place to go. I am shut out. Show me mercy!"

Now let me make a suggestion: I think that publican was Zacchaeus. Our Lord did not manufacture the story; it was the experience of an actual publican.

Jesus had already gotten the publican Matthew at the beginning of His ministry, and the only other publican whom we know He reached was this one here, Zacchaeus.

It is obvious that Zacchaeus is not satisfied, though he is rich. He is on a one-way street. He cannot stop; he has to keep going. But on the way he pauses and says, "O God, if there were only a mercy seat for me!"

Christ is moving now to Jerusalem, and on the way to the cross He stops to let that fellow know that there is a mercy seat for him and for all mankind.

And he sought to see who Jesus was, but could not because of the crowd, for he was of short stature.
(Luke 19:3)

I said at the beginning that there was a blind man when Jesus entered the city and a blind man when He left the city. You may have thought I was wrong, but Zacchaeus was the other blind man. He had sight, but his eyes were too close to the ground. He could not get them up high enough so he could look over the heads of the crowd to see Jesus. He wanted to see Him. Why?

Well, I'll tell you why. There was one ray of hope that penetrated this publican's soul. One day in the city of Jericho the word was passed along that the new Prophet from Galilee had chosen a publican by the name of Matthew to be one of His disciples. Further word was brought that the Prophet was receiving publicans and sinners, and that gave Zacchaeus a hope that he never expected to have. Therefore, when it was known that Jesus was coming through Jericho, Zacchaeus resolved to see Him. Zacchaeus said, "If I can, I'm going to get to Him because I want a mercy seat, I want salvation, I want to get to God."

Apparently, the Lord Jesus never did spend a night in Jericho, and He did not even linger there. He passed through hurriedly, and the crowds wanting to see Him lined the way. Now this little fellow Zacchaeus tried to penetrate the crowd but was unable to do so. He wanted to see Jesus. It was not idle curiosity, which is evident by the trouble he went to in order to see Him. It is obvious that this man was not satisfied with his life.

Zacchaeus was a success according to the world's standards. The standard of the world is that if a man gathers it all here and takes nothing with him after this life, he is successful; if he gathers it all for the next world and has nothing in this life, he is considered a failure. But wealth had not brought satisfaction to the soul of Zacchaeus. He wanted to go back to God. Could there be a way back for even a publican? What would this new Prophet say?

So he ran ahead and climbed up into a sycamore tree to see Him, for He was going to pass that way.
(Luke 19:4)

There has been a question regarding precisely what kind of tree it was. Some believe that it was a type of fig tree that grew in that area below sea level and was similar to a sycamore tree. However, I have some photographs of sycamore trees in present-day Jericho, and they look very much like the sycamore that grows here in Southern California. A sycamore tree has slick bark, and it is always a long way to the first limb. Since Zacchaeus was a little, short fellow, how I would like to have a picture of him shinnying up that tree! There are folk who do not see any humor in the Bible at all, but many of us find the Bible sprinkled with humorous situations. Here is one of them. It must have been a very comical sight to watch this little fellow climbing up into the sycamore tree to get a spot on the fifty-yard line, so to speak, in order that he might see Jesus.

After Zacchaeus had finally managed to reach the limbs and had concealed himself in the leaves, the Lord Jesus came along. When He was directly beneath Zacchaeus, one of the most remarkable things happened. Jesus stopped, looked up, and I think He laughed. Then I think Zacchaeus laughed, and all the tenseness of the scene was broken. You must recall that the Lord Jesus was human—oh, how human He was in dealing with the human family! Jesus said to him,

. . . Zacchaeus, make haste and come down, for today I must stay at your house.
(Luke 19:5)

That was like cool spring water on parched lips. It was the best news Zacchaeus had ever heard. No prophet, no man of God, ever had been willing to stop and speak to Zacchaeus, much less enter his home.

Who would be interested in the chief of publicans? Our Lord was.

If you think it was a struggle getting up in that tree, what do you think a little fellow coming down that slick trunk is going to do, especially when the Lord said, "Make haste"? He slid down the trunk and landed with a thud.

So he made haste and came down, and received Him joyfully.
(Luke 19:6)

Zacchaeus is rejoicing now. I think our Lord said to him, "Zacchaeus, I knew you all the time. I know what trouble you had getting up in that tree. And Zacchaeus, I knew when you went yonder to the temple where you had no right to go. I saw you stand afar off and beat your breast and cry, 'God be merciful to me a sinner!' Well, I have come to tell you that you, a publican, can have a mercy seat by which you can come back to God."

As they walked away together, notice the comments of the crowd:

But when they saw it, they all complained, saying, "He has gone to be a guest with a man who is a sinner."
(Luke 19:7)

You always have that crowd around—the critical, the self-righteous. The neighbors of Zacchaeus said, "He is a sinner." In that town he was known as a *sinner*—and

Jesus had entered his home as a guest! They were shocked beyond words.

Our Lord and Zacchaeus enter the house together, and the door shuts in our faces. I would like to gain entrance somehow and see what takes place, but the door is shut. We are outside with no keyhole reporter to get us any information. What does take place on the inside? I must confess that I do not know.

I do know this: After a lapse of time—perhaps an hour, two hours, three hours—the door opens.

Then Zacchaeus stood and said to the Lord, "Look, Lord, I give half of my goods to the poor; and if I have taken anything from anyone by false accusation, I restore fourfold."
(Luke 19:8)

Something happened on the inside. I do not know what was said, but the effect is revolutionary. Here is a man who has made his fortune by stealing, and that from his own people. His life has been devoted to one thing: getting all this world's goods that he could by any method. Now he says, "Lord, I am going to give half my goods to the poor; and if I have taken anything by false accusation, I'll restore it fourfold."

What happened? I am not sure exactly what took place, for the door was shut; but I want to make a suggestion. Our Lord in other interviews had allowed the conversations to be recorded, and in every recorded interview our Lord talked about man's sin and God's salvation. He talked about man's inability and God's ability. He talked about man's unworthiness and God's worthiness.

For instance, in the third chapter of John's Gospel, Jesus said to Nicodemus the Pharisee, "You must be born again." Nicodemus was incredulous, but Jesus insisted, "You must be born again. You have a need." Our Lord always mentioned man's need. Then He always talked about God's ability to meet that need. To Nicodemus He said, "And as Moses lifted up the serpent in the wilderness, even so must the Son of Man be lifted up, that whoever believes in Him should not perish but have eternal life" (John 3:14–15).

Also, sin and salvation were the subject in the encounter with the woman at the well. The Lord Jesus talked to her about her need, and how tactful He was as He pinpointed her sin! Then He identified Himself as the Messiah, the One who could meet her need.

You will find that He used this same procedure as He dealt with the blind men. Also, it is the way He dealt with His own disciples. It was His method.

Do you think He broke this pattern when He went into the home of Zacchaeus? I do not think so. He spoke to Zacchaeus about the fact that he was a sinner, and surely with Zacchaeus He did not have to labor that point. It is not so easy with the average church member who thinks that having his name on a church membership roll is all that is necessary for salvation. But Zacchaeus recognized that he was a sinner, and Jesus talked to him about His ability to meet the need of a sinner, even an outcast publican. I know that our Lord talked about salvation because when He came out of the house of Zacchaeus, He said, "Today salvation has come to this house. . . ."

We see a publican, a base sinner, this man Zacchaeus, step inside his house with the Lord Jesus Christ. The door shuts. The door opens, and this man steps out a new creation in Christ Jesus. He is not the same man who went in. We hear Zacchaeus say, "Lord [he calls Him *Lord*!], I'm going to give half my goods to the poor, and if I have taken anything by false accusation, I restore him fourfold."

FRUIT OF SALVATION

Someone says, "That is salvation by *works*." It is not. James writes, "But do you want to know, O foolish man, that faith without works is dead?" (James 2:20). James and Paul wrote about the same thing: Faith. James' emphasis is on the *works* of faith. You see, when James wrote he was saying simply this, "Men are justified by works, not the works of the law but the works of faith." And he was writing from man's viewpoint. When God sees us, He sees our hearts, and He knows whether or not we have saving faith. But when men see us, they don't see our hearts; they see the works of faith. And James says, "If the works of faith are not there, brother, you are not saved." Paul would agree with him, for Paul said practically the same thing.

Now let me repeat, I do not have Zacchaeus' confession of faith; I merely see the fruit of it. A secret session took place inside the Zacchaeus home, and I know nothing about it because the Holy Spirit has drawn a veil of silence over this interview. Ordinarily, the personal interviews which Jesus had are recorded in the Gospel record. This one is not recorded, and the reason is obvious. It is to set before us an illustration of faith being demonstrated and exhibited by *works*.

It is interesting to note that Zacchaeus did not come to the door of his home and say, "I want to give my testimony: Jesus saves and keeps and satisfies." Do not misunderstand me, a testimony is a wonderful thing if it is backed up with a life. It is a tragic thing when the life does not give credibility to the words.

Zacchaeus comes to the door and says, "Half my goods I will give to the poor, and I am going to start the rounds, making right the things that have been wrong." By his works I know he has been converted.

And that is the only way the world will know that you are converted. They do not know it by your testimony; they know it only by what they see in your life. Faith without works is dead, and faith with works is alive.

Neither did Zacchaeus come to the door of his home and say that he was going to join your church or my church. Oh, how many people today base their assurance of salvation upon church membership instead of upon a personal relationship to Christ! Zacchaeus revealed by his life that he had a personal relationship with Christ. The Word of God says that a believer is "created unto good works . . . adorned with good works . . . careful to maintain good works . . . zealous of good works . . . a pattern of good works." My friend, if good works are not in your life, faith in Christ must not be there. If it had not been for Zacchaeus' changed life, I would never have known that this old publican got converted.

Another thing I notice is that when Zacchaeus

opened the door of his home to Jesus, he did not adopt a particular label or declare himself to be a staunch defender of the faith. I'm not minimizing the importance of having our doctrine and our creed accurate, but the unforgiving spirit that is exhibited by many of our brethren today does not commend our position. The inability to confess our faults and to admit that there are occasions when we are wrong is certainly to be deplored. It is at this point that the great men of the past often make us look like spiritual pygmies. This was called to my attention some time ago in a rather peculiar experience.

The church I was serving at the time in Pasadena, California, had acquired a desk and a filing cabinet which formerly belonged to Dr. R. A. Torrey. The filing case was an old style one with envelopes—there must have been five hundred envelopes in this case. They were presumably empty, but one day I reached into it and took out an envelope by chance. There were two old letters in it. They were of a personal nature, and both were written by Frank DeWitt Talmage. I read them and discovered something of the bigness of these men of former days. Their bigness was revealed by their willingness to confess and correct a wrong. Surely there were "giants" in the earth in those days. A brief excerpt will reveal this trait which is so lacking in present-day Christian circles. The letter is dated January 2, 1900, and begins like this:

Dear Dr. Torrey:

Today I am standing under the shadows of two griefs: first that of Mr. Moody's death. Secondly, the fact that I may have done you a very great injustice. . . .

Then he confesses the wrong and names it, which we believe should not be done publicly even at this late date. We'll omit this portion of the letter but quote two more excerpts near the end:

If there is any way I can rectify the wrong, I will gladly do so. . . . May the sweet spirit of him who has gone make me more and more preach the gospel of love.

> Yours with sorrow,
> Frank DeWitt Talmage

Tears came to my eyes when I read these words which had been hidden from light for nearly half a century. It was startling to realize how far we had fallen even by mid-century—and how much more so now! We retain the traditions of biblical Christianity, but when was the last time you have seen such a sweet, humble, and quiet confession of wrong? We in Bible-believing circles seem to have the idea that if a man's head is screwed on right, his feet may go in any direction they want to go and he is still a child of God! My friend, when your head goes in one direction and your feet in another, something is radically wrong. Zacchaeus did not say that he was a Bible-believing Christian. He didn't have to say it, for he proved it by his works.

Listen again to the publican, that hardened sinner. He said, "Lord, I give half of my goods to the poor; and if I have taken anything from anyone by false accusation, I restore fourfold." And the next morning you could tell where Christ had stopped, you could tell which publican was trusting Christ by his actions! Zacchaeus did not go down to the office the next morning to continue his nefarious business; he set out to restore and to make right the things that were wrong. I can see the fruits of faith in the life of Zacchaeus. Therefore, I know the root is there.

THE PRINCIPLES INVOLVED

Now there are two great principles in this incident to which I should like to call your attention.

First of all, Christ must come into one's heart and life. That is essential. When a person comes to God, he must come as a sinner, as a beggar, bringing nothing and receiving everything. Oh, how that humbles us! It wounds our pride because we want to bring something, even if it is just a cup of cold water. But no good work makes any contribution to man's salvation!

Not by works of righteousness which we have done, but according to His mercy He saved us, through the washing of regeneration and renewing of the Holy Spirit. (Titus 3:5)

The Lord Jesus Christ knows you. Your sin is open scandal to Him, and He is well-acquainted with your need. He is the Savior who passed through this world about two thousand years ago to pay the penalty for your sin by His death on the cross. He stands at your door, prepared to meet the deepest need in your life. He awaits your invitation to enter.

The second great principle is that when Christ does come into the heart, a transformation is wrought. Zacchaeus never said anything about giving half of his goods to the poor the day before he climbed into that sycamore tree. But,

> **. . . if anyone is in Christ, he is a new creation; old things have passed away; behold, all things have become new.**
> (2 Corinthians 5:17)

My friend, you can tell where Christ has stopped. Until you let Him into your heart, there will be no real change in your life. Is your life a pattern of good works? If it is not, Christ is not there.

> **But do you want to know, O foolish man, that faith without works is dead?**
> (James 2:20)

8

SIMON PETER
Fisherman Afire

There are three well-marked periods in the life of Simon Peter, and they can be expressed like this: *Simon Peter at the fire, Simon Peter in the fire* (after he had failed so miserably), and *Simon Peter on fire;* that is, on the Day of Pentecost.

Now the first takes us to that fatal night in which our Lord was arrested out yonder in the Garden of Gethsemane and was rushed to trial that very night. Have you ever stopped to think how much of the Mosaic Law the religious rulers broke when they tried the Lord Jesus that night? They broke several, at least four, of their own precepts in trying Jesus for breaking their law! For instance, the Talmud said, "A criminal prosecution can neither commence nor terminate but during the day" yet they tried Him at night, which was strictly against their own laws. Then there was something else. No judgment was ever to be given on the eve of a Sabbath or a feast day, yet they brought in their judgment against Jesus that night before the great feast day. So you see that our Lord Jesus was tried in a very illegal manner.

Several attempts have been made to reenact the trial of the Lord Jesus and to bring these issues before the public again, letting them see how illegal His trial really was. An example of this is a little book that came into my hands when I was a seminary student. It was published years ago by a very prominent lawyer back East. I recall the interest that little book aroused among the students at that particular time.

Obviously, Jesus was betrayed by His own people. He was betrayed from the inside to the outside, and that is carried over to believers who are collectively called "the church." The church has always been hurt from the inside. In the past 1900 years there has never been an enemy on the outside of the church which has been able to harm it, to destroy it, or to defeat its purpose. The damage has always come from the inside. Our Lord was betrayed from the inside. Judas—one of His own, one of the twelve—betrayed Him to the religious rulers. The religious rulers betrayed Him to the mob, His own nation betrayed Him to the Romans, and the Romans nailed Him to the cross. He was betrayed from the inside to the outside, and that's the way it always goes.

Now there was another of His disciples, Simon Peter, who did an awful thing:

And Simon Peter followed Jesus, and so did another disciple [John]. Now that

disciple was known to the high priest, and went with Jesus into the courtyard of the high priest. But Peter stood at the door outside. Then the other disciple, who was known to the high priest, went out and spoke to her who kept the door, and brought Peter in. Then the servant girl who kept the door said to Peter, "You are not also one of this Man's disciples, are you?" He said, "I am not." Now the servants and officers who had made a fire of coals stood there, for it was cold, and they warmed themselves. And Peter stood with them and warmed himself.
(John 18:15–18)

SIMON PETER—WHO HE IS

On the night of the trial, Peter denied the Lord Jesus Christ there at the fire. But the very interesting thing is that all of his life he had been moving toward it. Have you ever stopped to think that no man in this life falls suddenly? Every now and then you hear of an outstanding man who all of a sudden does something that causes people to say, "I don't understand it. That man was such a tower of strength. He was so important in the community, and all of a sudden he's gone bad." However, no one goes bad suddenly. It's always a process. It always is something that has been working, gnawing, and eating away over a period of time.

I remember when I was pastor in Cleburne, Texas, there was a very prominent banker, an outstanding Christian layman—in fact, he was the one who sponsored the first tract that I ever wrote. He was very zealous, it seemed, for the things of the Lord. We left Cleburne but when I was back there for a visit, a friend told of how this man had robbed the bank where he was an officer. Actually, he almost caused the bank to go under because he held such an important position. Many people had entrusted everything they had into his hands, and they lost it all. Somebody made the statement, "He fell all of a sudden." No, he didn't. He didn't fall all of a sudden. When they checked back they found out that for years he had been falsifying records. He didn't go down suddenly. No man falls suddenly. It's always a gradual process. It's something that begins to eat away at the life until finally the break comes.

Likewise, Simon Peter all of his life had been gearing up for a fall. He had been moving toward the fire on that fateful night when he did this terrible thing. So let's go back in his life to that happy day when the Lord Jesus Christ was walking by the Sea of Galilee and saw these men who were fishermen. He called them, and one of them was Simon Peter. We are told that he left his net and followed the Lord.

But let's go back even further, even before our Lord saw Peter by the Sea of Galilee. It was probably beyond the Jordan River that Peter's brother Andrew came to him and said, "We have found the Messiah! We have met Him and talked with Him. I want to introduce you to the One who is the Messiah!" And Andrew brought his own brother Simon Peter to the Lord Jesus. It probably was the first time our Lord had ever seen him, and He said something to him that was quite unusual.

. . . **Now when Jesus looked at him, He said, "You are Simon the son of Jonah. You shall be called Cephas" (which is translated, A Stone).**
(John 1:42)

When our Lord said that, I think the crowd which was gathered there that day laughed. Do you know why they would laugh? They knew Peter. Under their breath they would say, "If He knew that fellow Simon Peter like we know him, He would never call him a stone. He would never talk about his being as stable as a rock wall. That fellow? Oh, you can't depend on him. He's unstable, he's vacillating, he's boastful, he's so cocksure, and yet he's always shifting. He's filled with conceit and ego." That's the man. They could laugh there that day, but our Lord didn't see him as he was. He saw beyond that to what He could make of Simon Peter.

And do you know, friend, that is what the Lord Jesus sees in you and sees in me. He doesn't see you as you are. He sees what He can do with you, what He can make out of you. That's the important thing. So those who thought they knew Simon Peter could laugh; but, may I say, it was the Lord Jesus who really knew this man.

Peter has been called the ignorant fisherman, but no man who spent three years in the school of Jesus could be called ignorant. And when we read Peter's epistles, we find he deals with important doctrine and handles very weighty subjects. In his first few verses he deals with the great doctrines of election, foreknowledge, sanctification, obedience, the blood of Christ, the

Trinity, the grace of God, salvation, revelation, glory, faith, and hope. My friend, you just couldn't have any more doctrine crowded into a few verses! The way in which he handles these great themes of the Bible reveals that he was by no means an ignorant man.

But Peter was an elemental soul. All of the basic qualities that go into human nature were in this man. He may even have been juvenile in some ways, possibly rude and crude, but he was never vulgar. He was a benevolent and lovable man. On the pages of Scripture we see him impulsive, often doing the wrong thing, but he's always doing *something*. He is a man of action. I like that kind of man.

As you know, there are a great many folk today in the church who everlastingly criticize everyone else. They never do anything themselves but sit on the sidelines. They are the ones who sit in the stands at the stadium and tell the quarterback how he *should* have called the signals.

An illustration of this is the time I went back to visit the college I had attended and went out to look at the old football field. I would have loved playing on the varsity, but I had to work and could never go out of town with the team. So I had to play with the second team. I remember one day we were giving the varsity a little practice, and believe me, they were roughing us up! One of the professors was sitting on the sideline, and every time we would make a play he would tell the fellow who was calling the signals how he should have done it. Finally this fellow just got tired, so he walked over to him and did something probably a student shouldn't do to a professor. He said, "Doctor, why don't you go get a uniform on and come out here and *show* us how to do it?"

May I say to you, there are a great many folks today who can tell you how to do it, but they don't do it themselves. Simon Peter was one of those lovable fellows who always was doing something. Chances are he would do it wrong but, thank God, he would do it. We need folks today like that who have a heart for the things of God and will make an attempt to do something for Him in these desperate days in which we are living. So this man Simon Peter was a man of action. That's the thing that characterized him.

Peter was a man who was daring and acted on impulse. He was filled with strange contradictions. For instance, after our Lord had fed the five thousand, He sent His disciples in a boat ahead of Him across the Sea of Galilee to the other side:

> **But the boat was now in the middle of the sea, tossed by the waves, for the wind was contrary. Now in the fourth watch of the night Jesus went to them, walking on the sea. And when the disciples saw Him walking on the sea, they were troubled, saying, "It is a ghost!" And they cried out for fear. But immediately Jesus spoke to them, saying, "Be of good cheer! It is I; do not be afraid." And Peter answered Him and said, "Lord, if it is You, command me to come to You on the water." So He said, "Come." And when Peter had come down out of the boat, he walked on the water to go to Jesus. But when he saw that the**

wind was boisterous, he was afraid; and beginning to sink he cried out, saying, "Lord, save me!" And immediately Jesus stretched out His hand and caught him, and said to him, "O you of little faith, why did you doubt?"
(Matthew 14:24–31)

Peter was impulsive. "Lord, if it is You, command me to come to You on the water." When the Lord said, "Come," he stepped right out of the boat! Think of that!

And may I say, Peter has certainly been criticized for this incident. They say he should not have asked to walk on water. Well, I rather admire the man for it. William Carey said, "Expect great things of God, and attempt great things for God." Certainly Peter did that! I'm afraid that most of us are satisfied with little things from God.

Notice also that Jesus did not rebuke Peter for asking. I hear people say that Peter failed to walk on the water. That is not the way my Bible reads. My Bible says that Peter *walked* on the water to go to Jesus. This is not failure! Peter asked a tremendous thing of God. No wonder God used him in such a wonderful way during the days that followed. No wonder he was chosen to preach the sermon on the Day of Pentecost!

Peter's problem that day was that he took his eyes off Jesus and looked at the boisterous waves. You and I are in the world today where we see the waves rolling, and this is the time we need to keep our eyes on the Lord Jesus Christ.

Peter was also a self-sacrificing man. "Then Peter said, 'See, we have left all and followed You'" (Luke 18:28). He left his nets, his business, all that he had. And when the Lord Jesus called him and said, "Follow Me and I'll make you a fisher of men," this man left everything and followed the Lord Jesus Christ. We need to be careful about criticizing him.

However, he was also self-seeking. We have the record of another occasion when Peter said to Him, "See, we have left all and followed You," and then added, "therefore what shall we have?" (Matthew 19:27). In other words, "I'd like to know what we will get out of it."

So Jesus said to them, "Assuredly I say to you, that in the regeneration, when the Son of Man sits on the throne of His glory, you who have followed Me will also sit on twelve thrones, judging the twelve tribes of Israel. And everyone who has left houses or brothers or sisters or father or mother or wife or children or lands, for My name's sake, shall receive a hundred-fold, and inherit eternal life."
(Matthew 19:28–29)

He was a self-seeking man and yet self-sacrificing.

Peter had spiritual insight. He said in John 6:68, "Lord, to whom shall we go? You have the words of eternal life." And yet he also had a spiritual stupidity:

From that time Jesus began to show to His disciples that He must go to Jerusalem,

and suffer many things from the elders and chief priests and scribes, and be killed, and be raised the third day. Then Peter took Him aside and began to rebuke Him, saying, "Far be it from You, Lord; this shall not happen to You!"
(Matthew 16:21–22).

In other words, "Lord, far be it from You to go to the cross and die. I just can't see that in Your program at all." He made two of the greatest confessions you'll find in the Gospels. The one that we've called to your attention, "Lord, to whom shall we go? You have the words of eternal life," and also Matthew 16:16, "You are the Christ, the Son of the living God." Yet he made the most cowardly denial.

SIMON PETER AT THE FIRE

Let's come to that final night. Watch him as he approaches the fire. The test begins early that evening. These are the things that lead us to the time when we fall and the time when we sin.

Proud

First of all, there is conceit in Simon Peter. Our Lord says, "One of you shall betray Me." Simon Peter looks at the other disciples, and he says in effect, "I've suspected this crowd all along, but there's one fellow here You can depend on; You can depend on me," and that man tries to prove it. He had gotten a sword that night and strapped it at his side. He not only intends to use it, he does use it. He intends to defend his Lord. He means every word he has said, but he fails because of conceit. He does not realize his own weakness. Pride and conceit always lead to a fall. This man does not realize how weak he really is—some of us have the same problem.

You may remember the little story I have told before about the young Scotch preacher who was in seminary. He was the most brilliant fellow in the class. And one day there was a call for an outstanding student to come and preach in one of the leading pulpits. So the seminary sent this boy because he was their finest student. He knew he was brilliant, and he had a notion that he would really shine that day. However, he had never spoken before the public and certainly not before that large a congregation. He didn't know about stage fright. So that Sunday morning he walked up into the pulpit with great pride and confidence; but when he began to preach, stage fright overcame him, and he forgot everything he knew. He stumbled badly all the way through. Finally he sat down in great embarrassment. A little Scotch lady sitting there was watching it all. After the benediction, when he had come down from the pulpit, she went up to him and said, "Young man, if you had gone up into that pulpit like you came down, you would have come down like you went up." May I say to you, many of us have learned the truth of Proverbs 16:18: "Pride goes before destruction, and a haughty spirit before a fall."

Oh, how strong this man Simon Peter felt on that fateful night. "These others may turn against You, but I'm one man You can depend on!"

Heedless

And there was the second step, the lack of alertness. Out yonder in the Garden of Gethsemane, our Lord took with Him the inner circle—Peter, James, and John—as He always did. They were the little babies, and you have to carry the babies, you know. He took them yonder, and He said to them, "You wait here while I go yonder and pray." And when He came back He found them asleep. In substance He asked them, "In an hour like this, couldn't you be alert?" I have noticed on the highways—especially on tollways— there are appearing these signs, "Be Alert," "Be Alert." And believe me, friend, you have to be alert today on the highways. There are two classes of people—the quick and the dead; and if you're not quick, you are dead! We hear today about so many accidents caused by drivers going to sleep at the wheel. Well, this man Simon Peter went to sleep at the wheel. He caused an awful wreck, the wreck of himself, if you please. It was a tragic thing.

Rash

Then we come to the third step of Peter's fall, the rashness of this man. That night when the soldiers came out, he drew his sword to use it! And he drew it without the Captain of his salvation giving any orders to do so. Well, you just don't draw a sword until the order comes from the one in command; but Simon Peter drew his. The rashness of this man!

Half-hearted

And then we come to the fourth step, and that is the half-heartedness of Peter. After our Lord was arrested, we are told that Peter followed Him afar off.

Those are the steps that lead to sin. Those are the steps that lead to the downfall of anyone.

Now will you notice Peter that night as he moves closer to the fire. He had gone with John to the palace of the high priest. John, we are told, knew the high priest, which means that he was well-known in those circles and had a pass. He got inside, but Peter had to stay outside. That night there were two fires and two groups. Outside there was a motley crowd around the fire, and Simon Peter had to stop there with that crowd. Then there was a gate, and at that gate was a serving maid. John had gotten by her and gone inside. Inside there was another fire, and standing around it was the brass. The officers, the religious rulers, the prominent people who were interested in the trial of Jesus, were there that night. So Simon Peter stayed outside, and John from within gives us this byplay: John saw that Simon Peter wasn't able to get in, so he went over and spoke to the officer in charge whom he knew. The officer then told John, "Yes, you can bring your friend in," so John went to the gate where the serving girl was. He called, and Peter came up talking, always talking. He had been talking outside to that crowd. My, how loquacious Peter was. He loved to speak, and this serving maid had been observing him. So when John asked to bring him inside, before she let him in she asked Peter the question, "You are not also one of this Man's disciples, are you?" And to the crowd on the outside, as he turned and looked back he said, "I am not." An awful thing to do! "I don't even know Him."

Now he moves to the inside where a fire is also burning. The brass, the elite crowd is there, but the crowd on the inside is more hostile to Jesus than the crowd on the outside. The crowd on the outside is just a mob—they will vote either way. But the crowd on the inside is in the know. They are the ones who hate Jesus. They are the ones who want Him crucified.

It is a cold night. Though it is springtime in Jerusalem, the nights are cold. Simon Peter elbows his way in among the brass, and moving into this crowd, he gets up closer to the fire. As he gets warm he starts talking again. He should not be talking to these folk. He's with the wrong crowd to begin with.

You know, friend, some crowds are wrong. I don't care what you say, there are some crowds you ought not to mingle with. Now don't misunderstand me, it is all right for John to be there. He would not deny Christ, but for Simon Peter to be there is wrong. That's the reason I believe that today we cannot put down one standard for all believers. I think that there are certain places some of us should avoid. If *you* go, it will be your downfall, while somebody else might go there and be unaffected. Simon Peter should not have stood with this crowd. These are the officials, and since Simon Peter seldom has the opportunity of speaking to the brass, he's telling them a few things.

It's a busy night. They're trying Jesus on the inside, and the soldiers are going back and forth. Another maid is busy performing her tasks, but as she comes by and hears this fellow speaking she says, "I remember him." She goes over to the maid who is stationed at the gate and asks, "That fellow over there doing all the talking, isn't he one of the disciples?" That maid says, "Yes, I think so. He denied it to me, but I'm sure he's one of the disciples." So this maid on the inside comes over to Peter and says, "You were with Him." Simon Peter denies it, "I was not with Him. I don't even know Him." It's an awful thing to have a little wisp of a maid cause you to deny your Lord! And then the whole crowd, including the hostile brass, look at him and begin to accuse him. They can see that he doesn't belong to them. An officer who is a relative of Malcus (the Malcus who was with the crowd that arrested Jesus in the garden, whose ear Peter had cut off) looks at Peter intently, and he says, "You *were* with Him." Peter becomes emotionally upset. He offers to take an oath. Think of that! "I'll take an oath that I do not even *know* that Man!"

And when Peter did that, I think a silence fell over the group; and out over the wall there was the breaking of the morning light, the first ray of the morning sun. Then in the silence there came the sound of a rooster crowing in the distance. When Simon Peter heard that, he realized what he had done.

SIMON PETER IN THE FIRE

Simon Peter is now *in* the fire. He had left the fire in the courtyard, but he's still in the fire. As he went out, he looked through that torch-lit judgment hall, and he caught the eyes of his Lord. His Lord did not rebuke him. I think the eyes of Jesus, the eyes of the One who had said, "I have prayed that your faith would fail not," were full of love and tenderness. The reason Peter did not commit suicide as Judas did was because of those words. He went out to mingle his tears with the dew on the hillside, to sob out his soul, and to wait for that moment when his Lord would come back from the dead.

Then came the day when Jesus did come back from the dead; and when He came back, Dr. Luke tells us that He appeared to Simon Peter. And Paul says that He appeared to Simon Peter privately. Why? They had business to transact. You see, every wrong thing a believer does has to be cleared up personally with Jesus Christ. You'll do it here, or you'll do it when you come into His presence. Simon Peter had to clean up his life, and he did. We have no record of that. Do you know why we have no record of it? Because "if we confess our sins, He is faithful and just to forgive us our sins and to cleanse us from all unrighteousness" (1 John 1:9). When God forgives, He doesn't keep talking about it, nor is it recorded. The thing that Peter had done was all straightened out between him and his Lord.

I've tried in my own mind to reenact how Simon Peter approached it. I think he told the Lord Jesus, "What a fool I've been these years! I'm always saying the wrong thing. I've had confidence in myself, and I had no right to have confidence in myself. I thought I'd be true to You, and I wasn't true to You. I betrayed You! Oh, I betrayed You, I betrayed You. And I want You to forgive me. I asked You one time to leave me and get someone else because I'm a sinful man. But now please don't leave me, I can never make it without You!" Our

Lord took that man back. I know He took him back because Peter is the man He chose to bring the first sermon on the Day of Pentecost.

This brings us now to Simon Peter *on* fire. We have seen Simon Peter *at* the fire. All of his life he had been moving toward that fire. It had to happen. If you keep toying and playing with sin, one of these days you will be burned by it and go down. Thank God, He will take you back if you will come back. And Simon Peter is in the fire until, repentant, he meets his resurrected Christ.

SIMON PETER ON FIRE

Now we pick up the story in the Book of Acts after the forty days post-resurrection ministry of Jesus. We see Simon Peter *on* fire when the Holy Spirit comes as the Feast of Pentecost is being celebrated. Allow me to lift out several verses that give us the events of the great Day of Pentecost, introduced by the coming of the Holy Spirit in a way that could both be seen and heard.

> **When the Day of Pentecost had fully come, they were all with one accord in one place. And suddenly there came a sound from heaven, as of a rushing mighty wind, and it filled the whole house where they were sitting. Then there appeared to them divided tongues, as of fire, and one sat upon each of them.**
> (Acts 2:1–3)

When the Holy Spirit came He was not visible. Through the ear-gate they heard the sound from heaven and through the eye-gate they saw the tongues that looked like fire resting on each of those believers present.

> **And they were all filled with the Holy Spirit and began to speak with other tongues [languages], as the Spirit gave them utterance.**
> (Acts 2:4)

This marked the beginning of the church. Ever since that day, every believer in the Lord Jesus is placed in the body of Christ by the agency of the Holy Spirit.

> **And when this sound occurred, the multitude came together, and were confused, because everyone heard them speak in his own language.**
> (Acts 2:6)

Jerusalem was crowded with people. They had come from everywhere because it was the Feast of Pentecost which every Jewish man was required to attend.

> **So they were all amazed and perplexed, saying to one another, "Whatever could this mean?" Others mocking said, "They are full of new wine."**
> (Acts 2:12–13)

I'm confident this amazing event had a tremendous effect not only on those who were in the church, but also on those who witnessed what took place, especially when they heard these men declaring in their own languages the mighty works of God. It was the annual celebration of the Feast of Pentecost in Jerusalem, and there were men and women from every corner of the Roman Empire speaking many different languages; yet each heard these new believers speaking in his own language. And they were, of course, bringing to them the wonderful news that "whoever calls on the name of the Lord shall be saved!"

Some were there who ridiculed. You always find that. Some mocked, and then we read;

But Peter, standing up with the eleven, raised his voice and said to them, "Men of Judea and all who dwell in Jerusalem, let this be known to you, and heed my words. For these are not drunk, as you suppose, since it is only the third hour of the day." (Acts 2:14–15)

The next twenty-five verses record this very marvelous sermon that Simon Peter brought on the Day of Pentecost. Now let's see the results of that sermon:

Now when they heard this, they were cut to the heart, and said to Peter and the rest of the apostles, "Men and brethren, what shall we do?" Then Peter said to them, "Repent, and let every one of you be baptized in the name of Jesus Christ for the remission of sins; and you shall receive the gift of the Holy Spirit. For the promise is to you and to your children, and to all

**who are afar off, as many as the Lord our
God will call." And with many other words
he testified and exhorted them, saying,
"Be saved from this perverse generation."
Then those who gladly received his word
were baptized; and that day about three
thousand souls were added to them.**
(Acts 2:37–41)

Will you notice that three thousand people were saved!
The reason that I do not sit in judgment on Simon
Peter is because of this sermon. Three thousand people
got saved! I am in no position to criticize any man who
can preach a sermon and three thousand people come
to a saving knowledge of Christ! Now maybe you are,
but I am not.

May I add something else? This is the reason I
have not criticized Billy Graham. I have a preacher
friend in San Francisco who is very critical of Billy
Graham, and I've almost lost the man's friendship
because I defend him. On one occasion I said to this
preacher, "When I see all these people coming to his
crusades in this Cow Palace and see when the invitation is given there are literally hundreds of people
coming to Christ, I can't criticize! I don't think you
and I together could get fifty people to come to the
Cow Palace to hear *us*! In fact, I don't think we could
get even fifty cows in there."

May I say, friend, this man Simon Peter had something unusual. As far as I know, no other man ever
had this experience. Any evangelist who is honest
will tell you that only a small percentage of his "con-

verts" stick; that is, experience genuine conversion. But three thousand people who listened to Simon Peter that day got saved, and they stuck. There has been no other message like this one in the history of the church. It's never been duplicated. You see, I don't criticize Simon Peter's sermons either. Simon Peter is now on fire!

A little later the religious rulers arrested Peter, and John with him.

And when they had set them in the midst, they asked, "By what power or by what name have you done this?" Then Peter, filled with the Holy Spirit, said to them, "Rulers of the people and elders of Israel: If we this day are judged for a good deed done to a helpless man, by what means he has been made well, let it be known to you all, and to all the people of Israel, that by the name of Jesus Christ of Nazareth, whom you crucified, whom God raised from the dead, by Him this man stands here before you whole. This is the 'stone which was rejected by you builders, which has become the chief cornerstone.' Nor is there salvation in any other, for there is no other name under heaven given among men by which we must be saved."
(Acts 4:7–12)

These men who knew Peter and what a coward he had been were aware of the things he had done and said. But we are told here that they perceived his boldness.

Now when they saw the boldness of Peter and John, and perceived that they were uneducated and untrained men, they marveled. And they realized that they had been with Jesus.
(Acts 4:13)

They perceived the *boldness* of this man.

From this time forward a great change is seen in the life of Peter. He had been impetuous, but now he is patient. He was bungling, fumbling, and stumbling when he first met Jesus. Our Lord told him in effect, "You are a weak man now, but I am going to make you a *Petros*, a rock-man." And Peter made it very clear that not he but the Lord Jesus is the Rock on which the church is built.

Simon Peter never takes an exalted position, as we see in his epistles. For instance, as he opens his first epistle, he calls himself an apostle—he's just one of them. Even though the Lord chose him to preach the first sermon on the Day of Pentecost, he did not feel that he was exalted above the others. But notice that whenever the names of the apostles were enumerated, Peter was always first on the list.

Although Peter deals with great doctrines and handles weighty subjects, he always writes in a warm manner. The great theme of the First Epistle of Peter is Christian hope in the time of trial. Hope is always tied in with suffering, and Peter has a great deal to say about the suffering of Christ and the suffering of Christ's own. Speaking out of his rich personal experience, while writing of suffering he emphasizes joy!

As a young preacher, I spoke a great deal about standing for the Lord and about suffering. I used to go to hospitals and pat people on the hand and pray with them. I would tell them that the Lord would be with them. At that time I was a professional preacher, saying what I did not know to be true from my own experience, although I believed it. But the day came when I went into the hospital myself. Another preacher came in and prayed with me. When he started to go, I said to him, "I've done the same thing you have done. I've been here, and I have told people that God would be with them. Now you are going to walk out of here, but I am staying; and I will find out if it is a theory or if what I have been telling people is true." I found it was true. Now it is no longer a mere theory for me. I know it not only by the fact that the Word of God says it but by the fact that I have experienced it!

What finally became of Simon Peter? Well, there are those who claim that they found Peter's bones in Rome. However, there is stronger evidence that his bones are somewhere else, probably down at Babylon. But Peter died a martyr as the Lord told him he would. Tradition says that when he was to be executed he made the request to be crucified head down, saying that he was not worthy to die with his head up as his Lord had died.

Simon Peter *at* the fire; Simon Peter *in* the fire; Simon Peter *on* fire. This is the fisherman who caught men. Tremendous isn't it?

Aren't you glad that when Peter denied the Lord, our Lord did not deny him? You and I are dealing with "the LORD [who] is gracious and full of compassion, slow to anger and great in mercy" (Psalm 145:8). He remains faithful even when we are faithless. He cannot deny Himself.

9

JUDAS ISCARIOT
Mystery of Iniquity
John 13:21–32

I trust that the lesson concerning this man may be very meaningful and valuable for each one of us.

> **When Jesus had said these things, He was troubled in spirit, and testified and said, "Most assuredly, I say to you, one of you will betray Me." Then the disciples looked at one another, perplexed about whom He spoke. Now there was leaning on Jesus' bosom one of His disciples, whom Jesus loved.**
> (John 13:21–23)

Let me interrupt to say that the disciple "Jesus loved" could have been any one of the disciples because our

Lord loved all of them. But one of them, the apostle John, claimed it; he was the one, of course, who wrote this Gospel of John.

> **Simon Peter therefore motioned to him to ask who it was of whom He spoke. Then, leaning back on Jesus' breast, he said to Him, "Lord, who is it?" Jesus answered, "It is he to whom I shall give a piece of bread** [called a sop] **when I have dipped it." And having dipped the bread, He gave it to Judas Iscariot, the son of Simon.**
> (John 13:24–26)

This gracious act of Jesus will mean more to us when we understand that it was an Eastern custom at meals for the host to offer one of his guests a morsel of tasty food, indicating special friendship. In this way our Lord was showing Judas His unconditional love for him.

> **Now after the piece of bread, Satan entered him. Then Jesus said to him, "What you do, do quickly." But no one at the table knew for what reason He said this to him. For some thought, because Judas had the money box, that Jesus had said to him, "Buy those things we need for the feast," or that he should give something to the poor. Having received the piece of bread, he then went out immediately. And it was night. So when he had gone out, Jesus said, "Now the Son of Man is glorified, and God is glorified in Him. If**

**God is glorified in Him, God will also glo-
rify Him in Himself, and glorify Him
immediately."**
(John 13:27–32)

This brings before us the most unsavory character of
history! Judas, mystery of iniquity. Many thought that
when the Messiah came the first time He would institute the Kingdom, that He would remove sin and iniquity from the earthly scene. Even the apostles
tenaciously held on to that view after the resurrection,
for they asked Him the question, "Lord, will You at this
time restore the kingdom to Israel?" (Acts 1:6).

And some today stubbornly believe that Jesus did set
up His Kingdom the first time He came and that iniquity is dying out on the earth! I was amazed to read the
message given by a leading liberal at one of the World
Council meetings. He had the temerity and the audacity to say that, although conditions were bad in certain
areas and sections of the world, actually as we inch
back a little, we always move forward a foot or two! For
the life of me I could not understand how we were moving forward a foot or two when he gave no illustration
of that or proof for making such a statement.

Scripture teaches the contrary. The Word of God
teaches very clearly that iniquity would abound more
and more. Our Lord gave mystery parables which
would reveal the course of this age in which we live,
and He told about darnel—tares, if you please—that
were sown in the wheat fields. He said that the tares
would grow along with the wheat and would head up

and become full even for a harvest. Certainly that is true. And after two thousand years, it is obvious.

The Lord Jesus also gave the parable of leaven. Leaven would be hidden in three measures of meal by a woman, and it would finally work and work in its corrupting influence until the entire three measures of meal were corrupted and leavened. This was the picture our Lord gave.

It was the apostle Paul who wrote to Timothy, the young preacher, and said to him in 2 Timothy 3:13, "But evil men and impostors will grow worse and worse, deceiving and being deceived." And when Paul wrote one of his first epistles to the believers in Thessalonica, he said,

> **For the mystery of lawlessness is already at work; only He who now restrains will do so until He is taken out of the way. And then the lawless one will be revealed, whom the Lord will consume with the breath of His mouth and destroy with the brightness of His coming.**
> (2 Thessalonians 2:7–8).

So the intent and content of the Word of God is that iniquity would abound and that evil men would abound, becoming worse and worse. The human race has had a long and sordid history of iniquity, for the mystery of iniquity has been working from the very beginning. We begin with Cain who slew his brother. We move down to Nimrod, who was a hunter of the souls of men. Esau, the man of the flesh who even sold his birthright for a little bowl of stew, did so not because he was starving but because he despised the birthright and attached no value to that which God said was extremely important. And down through the centuries we have had Pharaoh, who could outdo Eichmann in killing off the nation Israel; Ahab and Jezebel, the wicked king and queen of Israel; and moving on down we come to Nebuchadnezzar; then there was Haman who made a gallows to kill Mordecai and then set out to slay all the people of Israel; and there was Antiochus Epiphanes who profaned the temple; and then Herod who slaughtered the little ones in an effort to kill the Christ child. Pilate handed in the sentence of death against the Lord Jesus Himself; Titus the Roman leveled Jerusalem; and Nero began the persecution of Christians in the Roman Empire and executed Paul the apostle. There were also the popes of the inquisition who literally killed thousands of believers as well as Jews; and Hitler carried on this sordid story; and the ruthless Marxists who have headed Communism in our day.

Certainly the mystery of iniquity is working in the world, but none in this catalog of infamy is more outstanding or infamous than the man of sin who is called Judas. Up to the present, Judas epitomizes the "man of sin" who will finally appear in the world.

Now the reason that I do not understand him is very simple, and I think that it may be the reason you do not understand him. Let me use the illustration which I used on our television program at one time. I told the viewers I was holding behind me a stick which was straight, and I asked that they visualize that stick.

Then I pulled it out and let the audience see it. I said to them, "Every one of you visualized this stick exactly as it is because it can be straight in only one way." Then I said, "I have another stick here that is crooked, and I ask that you visualize this stick that is crooked." Then when I pulled that stick out I said, "I have a notion that not one of you visualized this stick as it really is because it is really a very crooked one." It could be crooked in a hundred different ways, but it can be straight in only one way.

You see, goodness is simple. It is evil that is complicated. That's one of the reasons life is so complicated for many of us today. We are frustrated and go off on a tangent because of the fact that we let evil come into our lives; and when it does, it brings complications. In contrast, goodness is always simple. You can go straight in only one direction, but you can go crooked in a million directions. For this reason Judas is a man difficult to understand. You do not know just which way he will step the next time.

Now there are some things that we do know about him, and they are biographical. Those are the things we want to look at now. It would take a separate message to talk about him psychologically—the motives that were in that man's heart. What was it that prompted him to betray Jesus? But now I am merely dealing with the facts that are given in the Bible and seeing only what the Word of God has to say.

Let's pick up his story in John, chapter 6, as it is given to us:

He spoke of Judas Iscariot, the son of Simon, for it was he who would betray Him, being one of the twelve.
(John 6:71)

This man was the son of Simon Iscariot, and he originally came from Kerioth which is in Judah. This means Judas alone of all the apostles was not a Galilean. He, like the Lord Jesus Himself, was from the tribe of Judah. His background was good. He had fine family connections. You never would have seen his picture in the ten most wanted criminals that the FBI puts out. He just didn't mingle with that crowd at all. This man had a marvelous heritage. Also he had physical qualifications. Probably he was attractive. I think he was even handsome, very much like one of his predecessors, Saul, Israel's first king. Saul was a tall fellow, ". . . From his shoulders upward he was taller than any of the people," we are told in 1 Samuel 9:2. Samuel loved him because he looked like a king. And Samuel did not go along with the Lord's decision when He said, "I have rejected him from reigning over Israel." Samuel couldn't see it. Saul was too attractive to be rejected. Judas Iscariot was probably the most physically attractive of all the apostles. And I believe he was suave, sophisticated, and polished. Also he was clever, and he was sharp. He was different from the Galileans. Certainly he was not like Peter; nor was he like John or Philip. He was not like these untrained men who had come down from Galilee. This man Judas happened to be among those in the upper bracket. May I put it like this: He probably looked more like an apostle than any other apostle. More than likely, you would have chosen him above all others; and the remarkable thing about this man is that even to the last minute, not one of the other apostles suspected Judas.

Have you ever noticed that the man who goes wrong is the man whom you would least suspect? Someone this past week said to me concerning a man who was known to us mutually, "That's the last man I ever thought would go wrong." And neither did anyone suspect Judas. When our Lord in the Upper Room said, "One of you shall betray Me," no one turned and looked at Judas and said, "There he is!" I'll tell you what each one of them did say: "Is it I?" May I pause to say this, if you have not discovered that there is a Judas in you, you do not know yourself. Every apostle—Peter, John, Andrew, Philip—asked, "Is it I?" Why did they say that? Because each man knew he was capable of denying Christ. And, my friend, may I make a confession today—and please let's not let this get out—if it were not for the grace of God I would deny Him in the next five minutes. I am thankful for His grace! Aren't you thankful for the grace of God which has saved you and *kept* you? There's just a little of Judas in all of us. "Lord, is it I?" Nobody pointed a finger at this man and said, "There he is, he's the rascal," because nobody thought he was the rascal.

When Leonardo da Vinci painted his conception of the Last Supper, naturally he had difficulty getting a man to pose as his model for Christ. He finally found that man. Then he had a harder job than that. He couldn't find anyone to pose for the person of Judas. He waited and searched. Finally, years later he found the evil face he wanted, scarred by years of sin. It was the same man who before had posed for the person of Christ!

But the interesting thing is, friend, Leonardo da Vinci was a great artist, but he did not know Judas. Judas looked like the man who had posed for the figure of Christ. He *looked* like an apostle. Nobody suspected him. He's the one who was trusted by all the other apostles. They elected him their treasurer, and yet John says he was a thief. I do not know where or when John got that information. Perhaps Judas had a past record discovered after his death; we do not know, but we have the information in John 12:6 that Judas was a thief.

Again, I'm not exploring the psychological aspects of this man, but it is interesting to study the way crime has moved down through the lives of men. I have always felt it is valuable to my ministry to know the background of individuals who have become criminals, and I have attempted to read everything I could in this field. That's the reason I like to read detective stories, but of late they have become so sorry that they're not worth reading. The authors all use the same plot now, and the stories are all running the same way. However, I remember years ago reading the story of Gaston B. Means, who spent most of his latter life in Leavenworth Prison. He is remembered for his connection with the Lindbergh kidnapping case. He got his finger on everything. This man was one of the biggest criminals and crooks our country has ever had. Everywhere he went, he was trusted. He was a bespectacled, pudgy fellow and very dignified looking. In every town in

which he lived he was elected the Sunday school super-
intendent, and he was made the Scout Master of the
Boy Scout troop. He served in those capacities in town
after town until they found out about him. It is interesting to note men like that. Judas Iscariot was that
kind of man. He could live day and night among the
apostles and not be discovered. That's amazing! For
three years those men were close to him, yet he never
revealed his true nature.

Now will you notice some remarkable insights from
the Word of God.

> **But Simon Peter answered Him, "Lord, to
> whom shall we go? You have the words of
> eternal life. Also we have come to believe
> and know that You are the Christ, the Son
> of the living God." Jesus answered them,
> "Did I not choose you, the twelve, and one
> of you is a devil?"**
> (John 6:68–70)

That word *devil* is not *demon* but actually *devil*, meaning a slanderer. Judas was a clever gossip.

> **He spoke of Judas Iscariot, the son of
> Simon, for it was he who would betray
> Him, being one of the twelve.**
> (John 6:71)

Now there are two problems that are raised by this
statement, and we're going to deal with them briefly.
First, if it was determined previously and prior to his
birth that Judas was to betray Christ, should we hold

him responsible for what he did? Isn't he more to be pitied than to be censured? And second, why did Jesus choose Judas in the first place if He knew what he was going to do? I remember hearing the answer of the great Dr. Joseph Parker of London when someone came to him and asked, "Why did Jesus choose Judas?" He said, "That's a question that is difficult to answer, but I can give you one that is more difficult than that. Why did Jesus choose me?" And, my friend, why did Jesus choose you? That's a bigger question than why He chose Judas. And if you will answer why He chose you, then I will answer why He chose Judas.

However, I want to explore these problems with you briefly. Judas has the questionable distinction of being the only apostle mentioned in prophecy and, by the way, he is mentioned in several places. I turn to only one:

Even my own familiar friend in whom I trusted, who ate my bread, has lifted up his heel against me.
(Psalm 41:9)

He is not mentioned there by name; but may I say to you, even if he had been mentioned by name, it would not necessarily have been Judas Iscariot, because there were two men named Judas among the apostles. If you had been there and had looked them over, you probably would have picked the other Judas as being the one to betray the Lord Jesus. Therefore, my friend, even if he had been called by name, he still did not have to be the one mentioned in this psalm.

Another thing to notice is that there is no mention of Judas' call. The Scripture records the call of Peter and Andrew, Philip and Nathanael, and the call of Matthew; but we do not find the call of Judas. This has prompted some to say that he intruded into this position—forced his way into the apostolate. It is true that after Judas left the Upper Room the Lord Jesus did say to the other men, "You did not choose Me, but I chose you. . . ." (John 15:16). May I say also, go back to John 6:70, which I have already called to your attention: "Jesus answered them, 'Did I not choose you, the twelve, and one of you is a devil?'" Our Lord had said, even before Judas left the group, that He had chosen them. We know that Judas, of his own free will, made his choice to continue with Jesus because in this same incident many of His disciples went back and no longer walked with Christ. Then our Lord turned to those whom He had chosen and said to the twelve, "Do you also want to go away?" (John 6:67). Any one of the twelve could have walked away, but Judas did not walk away because he willed not to walk away. He stayed. Why? I cannot answer that, but he did stay although he could have left.

Now this man exercised his free will, and we do not see him brought into prominence until we come to the time when our Lord is moving to the cross. In the light of the cross, Judas stands as a dark silhouette on the horizon. I want you to notice several statements concerning this man which may help us understand him just a little bit.

It was in Bethany in the home of Lazarus, Mary, and Martha—a place where Jesus was loved—that they made Him a dinner. It was the last act of love that was shown to Him. The apostles were guests also, and Mary entered into His suffering by doing a lovely thing:

> **Then Mary took a pound of very costly oil of spikenard, anointed the feet of Jesus, and wiped His feet with her hair. And the house was filled with the fragrance of the oil.**
> (John 12:3)

The fragrance of it not only filled that room but has filled the world since then. Notice what happened:

> **But one of His disciples, Judas Iscariot, Simon's son, who would betray Him, said, "Why was this fragrant oil not sold for three hundred denarii and given to the poor?" This he said, not that he cared for the poor, but because he was a thief, and had the money box; and he used to take what was put in it.**
> (John 12:4–6)

You see this man expressing an interest in the poor, and certainly the Old Testament had taught him that. Psalm 41:1 says, "Blessed is he who considers the poor. . . ." Judas said, "Why wasn't this given to the poor?" But the Lord Jesus rebuked him, and I feel sure it was a gentle rebuke. Jesus said, "Let her alone; she has kept this for the day of My burial. For the poor you have with you always, but Me you do not have always" (John 12:7–8). The interesting thing is that Judas

Iscariot is revealing his true nature. This man could not stand to be rebuked. He was highly incensed; he would not be reprimanded. His attitude was definitely bad, and it's probably the thing that prompted him to betray our Lord for thirty pieces of silver. Apparently the thing that motivated him was money.

Now as the events progress we find that Judas' agreement with the chief priests and captains was that some time after the feast he would betray the Lord. So he leisurely returned to the group, and when they went into the Upper Room he was reclining there with the others:

> **And supper being ended, the devil having already put it into the heart of Judas Iscariot, Simon's son, to betray Him, . . .**
> (John 13:2)

He's just waiting for the opportunity and the moment. He's in no hurry. Finally the Lord Jesus forces his hand. It's the only time that our Lord closed in on this man and forced him to act. Up to this time Judas was perfectly free to go and come as he willed, but now the Lord Jesus pressures him.

> **Now after the piece of bread, Satan entered him. Then Jesus said to him, "What you do, do quickly."**
> (John 13:27)

He went out immediately and contacted those with whom he had bargained. I surmise that he told them,

"I've been discovered! He knows that I'm to betray Him, and if you are going to arrest Him you'll have to do it this night. I know where He's going, and if you will go with me, we can get Him tonight." So immediately they went out to take the Lord Jesus. You see that Judas made a deliberate choice. It was a choice made for time and eternity. And it was a choice that he was free to make. First we find Judas being blinded by Satan, blinded by his anger, blinded by his rebellion. This man had no notion of yielding to Jesus Christ. Having been blinded by Satan, he belongs to Satan; and from here on he will do Satan's bidding. Therefore, Jesus forced his hand. But notice that even at the last minute our Lord still gave Judas an opportunity. After our Lord's agonizing prayer in the Garden of Gethsemane He came again to the sleeping disciples and said,

"Rise, let us be going. See, My betrayer is at hand." And while He was still speaking, behold, Judas, one of the twelve, with a great multitude with swords and clubs, came from the chief priests and elders of the people. Now His betrayer had given them a sign, saying, "Whomever I kiss, He is the One; seize Him." Immediately he went up to Jesus and said, "Greetings, Rabbi!" and kissed Him. But Jesus said to him, "Friend, why have you come?" Then they came and laid hands on Jesus and took Him.
(Matthew 26:46–50)

We see that our Lord gave Judas an eleventh-hour reprieve. He gave him another opportunity when he came out and kissed Him. The Lord Jesus, who knew why Judas had come, said to him, "Friend, why have you come?" In other words, "It is not too late for you to change your motive and to change your attitude. It's not too late for you to change that hot kiss of betrayal into a kiss of acceptance." But Judas would not accept the opportunity. And even after that incident in Gethsemane, our Lord gave him still another chance!

When morning came, all the chief priests and elders of the people plotted against Jesus to put Him to death. And when they had bound Him, they led Him away and delivered Him to Pontius Pilate the governor.

Now will you notice,

Then Judas, His betrayer, seeing that He had been condemned, was remorseful and brought back the thirty pieces of silver to the chief priests and elders, saying, "I have sinned by betraying innocent blood." And they said, "What is that to us? You see to it!"
(Matthew 27:1–4)

Now Judas was given a final opportunity. He came to these priests, who had the Lord Jesus with them at the very time. Why didn't Judas go to Christ? Why didn't he turn to Him and say to Him, "Will You forgive me?" And our Lord would have forgiven him. But he did not turn to the Lord Jesus Christ, though He was right there in the crowd, bound and on the way to the cross. The repentance of Judas was that of the average thief who has been caught and repents—not because he stole, but because he has been caught! And that's the repentance of Judas. Though He had been given several opportunities, he did not turn to Christ at all. Instead, what did he do? Judas went out and committed suicide. According to Acts 1:18, either the rope broke or someone cut him down so he would not be hanging there during the feast day. He died for his own sin while Jesus died on the cross for him! Judas would not have Jesus but turned his back on Him and paid the penalty for his own sin.

Now what is the enormity of this man's crime? He's more than just a conscience-stricken man. Dante put Judas and Brutus in the lowest place in *The Inferno*. I think he missed the import of this man's crime. I want you to consider something very carefully, and it's this: There were certain sins in the Old Testament which were called sins of ignorance, and also there were sins of presumption. Notice them. Sins of ignorance are mentioned in Hebrews 9:7:

But into the second part the high priest went alone once a year, not without blood, which he offered for himself and for the people's sins committed in ignorance.

The great Day of Atonement was when a lamb or a goat was offered and the blood was brought into the Holy of Holies to recognize the fact that these people had a sin nature.

My friend, whether or not you know you are a sinner, you *are* one. A missionary came to Dr. Hudson Taylor who had been talking to his young missionary recruits about the fact they were sinners. This young fellow had the audacity to say, "Dr. Taylor, I do not feel as though I am a sinner." Dr. Taylor looked at him and said, "Young man, God says you are a sinner. Take it by faith, you are a sinner." Beloved, there are sins of ignorance. You and I are sinners whether we know it or not. And a great many people in your community are sinners in ignorance today. They do not know the enormity of their crime.

In the Old Testament there was a sacrifice that could be offered for the sins of ignorance. But there was another sin for which there was no atoning sacrifice; that was for presumptuous sins. Listen to David, if you please.

Who can understand his errors? Cleanse me from secret faults. Keep back Your servant also from presumptuous sins; let them not have dominion over me. Then I shall be blameless, and I shall be innocent of great transgression.
(Psalm 19:12–13)

There is no sacrifice for sins of presumption. If a man was murdered in Israel, the murderer was stoned to death because it was a deliberate, premeditated thing; and there was no sacrifice for that.

Now listen to David when he went in to confess his sin; and, friends, his sin was a presumptuous sin! He murdered Uriah by assigning him to the forefront of the hottest battle. David knew Uriah would be killed, and he was. David had committed adultery with Uriah's wife, and then he committed murder to cover himself. This was a presumptuous sin, but listen to David:

For You do not desire sacrifice, or else I would give it; You do not delight in burnt offering. The sacrifices of God are a broken spirit, a broken and a contrite heart— these, O God, You will not despise.
(Psalm 51:16–17)

David realized that he could bring no sacrifice for his sins. But he came to God with a broken and a contrite heart to confess them. He cast himself upon God's mercy, and God forgave him.

Judas could have done the same. Although he committed a presumptuous sin, he could have cast himself upon Christ and been forgiven. We read in Psalm 2:12, "Kiss the Son, lest He be angry, and you perish in the way. . . ." Judas kissed the Son of God, and the Lord Jesus said to him, "Friend, why have you come?" It was not too late. Even at that moment Judas could have turned that evil kiss of betrayal into the humble acceptance of Christ. "Kiss the Son, lest He be angry, and you perish in the way."

Over in the Book of Hebrews there is a very clear statement regarding presumptuous sin, and I'll close with this verse,

For if we sin willfully after we have received the knowledge of the truth, there no longer remains a sacrifice for sins.
(Hebrews 10:26)

The worst thing in the world is to hear the clear presentation of the gospel and turn your back on Jesus Christ. That is a presumptuous sin. That was Judas' sin. There is no remedy for that sin.